The University of Tennessee, Memphis
College of Nursing

From Diploma to Doctorate:

Years of Nursing

BY E. DIANNE GREENHILL, RN, BSN, EdD

PROFESSOR OF NURSING

with contributions from

VIRGINIA TROTTER BETTS '69

BEVERLY H. BOWNS, FACULTY

MARIE BUCKLEY '37

MICHAEL A. CARTER, DEAN

CHERYL L. COX '70

CAROLYN DEPALMA '56

VERNON TOWNSLEY HARGETT '45

MARGARET HARTIG '77, '93

MARY HARTWIG '93

DONNA HATHAWAY, FACULTY

VIRGINIA HARPER JONES '45

JEANETTE LANCASTER '66

JUNE LARRABEE '92

JUDY C. MARTIN '88, '94

MARGARET NEWMAN '62

MILDRED B. PROCTOR '28

MARY LOU SHANNON '59

PHYLLIS SKORGA '71, '76

CHERYL CUMMINGS STEGBAUER '69, '94

JIMMIE MACDONALD WRIGHT '45

ORIGINALLY PUBLISHED BY THE UNIVERSITY OF TENNESSEE, MEMPHIS, 1998

UT Memphis College of Nursing
877 Madison Avenue.
6th Floor Lamar Alexander Building
Memphis, TN 38163
901-448-6128

AUTHOR:
E. Dianne Geenhill

EDITOR
Lori Brougher

DESIGNER
Geri Meltzer

100TH ANNIVERSARY BOOK COMMITTEE
E. Dianne Greenhill, chair
Carolyn DePalma
Cheryl Stegbauer
Jimmie Wright

SPECIAL THANKS TO
Kathy Stewart
Lillian Wells
Mary Lou Wilson
All the faculty and alumni who provided photos, article and support

The University of Tennessee is an EEO/AA/TitleIX/Section 504/ADA Institution.
R07-3801-39-001-98

Table of Contents

UTHSC in 2015 —
Message from the Chancellor

BY STEVE J. SCHWAB, MD

Robert F. Kennedy, politician and U.S. Attorney General, once stated, "Few will have the greatness to bend history itself; but each of us can work to change a small portion of events, and in the total; of all those acts will be written the history of this generation."

The thousands of women and men who are graduates of the UT College of Nursing and who have served as faculty and staff in the college are proud of the many acts undertaken through the years, which are chronicled in this comprehensive centenary book. Together, your myriad contributions have propelled nursing forward in the arenas of patient care, education, research and community service. For that we are most grateful. In particular, we extend our gratitude to one of our own nursing professionals, Dianne Greenhill, RN, BSN, EdD, who made a personal commitment to painstakingly research and accurately retell how the UT College of Nursing was established and evolved through its first century.

The historical evidence is clear. Those who choose the nursing profession possess an innate desire to make a positive difference in every life they touch. Such is the root of the nursing profession. To achieve their goals, nurses collaborate, innovate, analyze, re-imagine and persevere, working in partnership with health care professionals from a wide range of disciplines to constantly elevate standards of care. What has been true for the college's first 100 years continues to ring true today. Nurses make a difference in all the right ways.

As UTHSC presses forward with today's major initiatives, the choices we make now are the ingredients for tomorrow's history. The College of Nursing remains a pivotal UTHSC component and will doubtless continue to make substantive contributions to our organization's story. One element of the Campus Master Plan entails planning a permanent home for the college with facilities that will allow for future expansion as health care needs demand. Our institutional commitment to the college also translated into paving the road for Nursing's expansion in the Nashville area, as we build a full-fledged UTHSC campus in the capitol to serve middle Tennessee.

We thank you for your pride in and active support of the UT College of Nursing. And in the words of Marge Piercy, novelist, poet and memoirist — "Never doubt that you can change history. You already have."

Steve J. Schwab, MD
Chancellor
UTHSC

Message from the Chancellor

BY WILLIAM R. RICE, JD, CHANCELLOR, UT MEMPHIS AND
VICE PRESIDENT FOR HEALTH AFFAIRS, UNIVERSITY OF TENNESSEE

The 100th anniversary of the College of Nursing at The University of Tennessee, Memphis provides all of us in the UT family with a special time to remember and to celebrate the achievements of the faculty, students and staff who have been a part of the College throughout the first century of its existence.

William R. Rice, JD
Chancellor
UT Memphis

During this time, the College of Nursing has gained a reputation for always being at the forefront in innovative nursing education, for producing graduates who have served the citizens of our state and our nation with distinction, and for advancing nursing as an increasingly important health profession. Begun as a hospital-based nursing school in 1898, the College of Nursing today has taken its place as a full partner in the education, research and service missions of the University of Tennessee.

This book chronicles the development of the College of Nursing, both through the presentation of factual information about the College's history and through the perspectives of distinguished faculty and alumni of the College. The book's author, Dr. Dianne Greenhill, has been on the faculty of the College since 1965. Dr. Greenhill's keen interest in the College's history, her love of the nursing profession and her skill as a writer have provided us with an important document that will be treasured by all those who have been or will be associated with the College of Nursing. The University of Tennessee is greatly indebted to Dr. Greenhill for writing this book, and I personally applaud and congratulate her for this fine accomplishment.

Forward

BY MICHAEL ALLEN CARTER, DNSc
DEAN, UT MEMPHIS COLLEGE OF NURSING

The College of Nursing has been an important part of the health care for Memphis and the Midsouth since the very early days. In many ways, our history has been tied to the determination and vision of some very strong women. Beginning with the early efforts of Lena Angevine Warner, through the merger with the University of Tennessee Medical Units, and during the gifted leadership of Ruth Neil Murry, the College blended the education of future nurses with the important leadership in clinical practice.

Michael Allen Carter, DNSc
Dean, UT Memphis
College of Nursing

In the early days, the curriculum was difficult. There were long hours and working conditions that left much to be desired. The faculty and students lived through and were sometimes participants in wars, epidemics, and social upheaval. Throughout all of these challenges, the College built its reputation on the outstanding achievements of its graduates.

Today, it is difficult to understand the requirements of earlier days. For example, few students of today would kneel before the Dean to have a cap placed on their head. Also, few would tolerate the daily measurement of hems from the floor. With the diverse student body we see today, we find it amusing that earlier students were required to be white women of average height and weight.

We have much to learn from our history as a College of Nursing. And, all of us are deeply indebted to those earlier faculty and students who blazed the trails we tread today. We stand in view of our second century of history with challenges ahead that could not be imagined by those who helped us get here. I have great faith that the second 100 years will have as many achievements as have our first 100 years. I also have great faith that tomorrow's students and faculty will meet the challenges as in the past and will continue to make our College the national treasure it is.

Message from the Current Dean 2015

BY WENDY LIKES, PhD, DNSc, APRN-BC
RUTH NEIL MURRY ENDOWED CHAIR

Nursing has served as a cornerstone of the Memphis health care delivery system since the Civil War (1861 to 1865). The story of our profession is inextricably intertwined with the growth and development of this singularly different city and the Midsouth region. At every major turning point of the Memphis story where health care touches history, nurses are there — contributing as learners, leaders and lifesavers.

Wendy Likes,
PhD, DNSc, APRN-BC
Dean, UT Memphis
College of Nursing

For me and many of my colleagues, nursing was a calling, a compulsion of the very best kind — to serve others and to heal. As you enjoy the retelling of nursing history in this book, there will doubtless be many occasions when you recognize that same irresistible calling that propelled these historical figures to take action.

Today, nurses continue to answer the call. We play a pivotal role as a linchpin in the rapidly evolving health care system. More than at any other time, nurses are challenged to do more and be more for our patients, employers, and families of those in our care. Simultaneously, we must also strive to connect more closely with our health care colleagues; to establish and maintain methods of operating that revolve around and enhance team care. Since technological and societal changes unfurl at a blazing pace and what is revolutionary today can be obsolete or routine in six months, it is more important than ever to take time to pause, reflect and examine just how far we and our profession have come. For we can best plot a successful course for the future, through a thorough understanding of our past.

And while our profession's growth and advances are chronicled here with insight, wisdom and an unfettered realism, these stories also capture and highlight aspects of nursing from yesteryear that are part of who we are as nurses today — compassion, ingenuity, courage, dedication and hopefulness. These are ties that bind all healers who accept the responsibilities of the nursing profession. I have great faith these same attributes will be reflected in generations of nurses to come.

Introduction

BY E. DIANNE GREENHILL, EdD
PROFESSOR, UT MEMPHIS COLLEGE OF NURSING

The University of Tennessee, Memphis College of Nursing has a rich heritage beginning with one of the earliest diploma or certificate programs in Tennessee and continuing with the first nursing doctoral program in the state. This book chronicles the 100 year history and includes perspectives of both alumni and faculty.

Writing the College of Nursing's history was the dream of Ruth Neil Murry. When illness prevented her from realizing this goal, the "dream" was passed to me, a former student. I had the privilege and opportunity to spend many hours with Miss Murry researching, listening, and sharing ideas.

The book took form when planning began for our 100th anniversary in 1998. Dean Michael Carter appointed a committee to develop the publication. Carolyn DePalma, Cheryl Stegbauer, and Jimmie Wright served on this committee reviewing the proposed outline, narrative and assisted in picture selection. I am grateful for their valuable assistance in planning, as well as contributing pictures and articles.

It is an impossible task to write a complete history, especially for a span of 100 years. While Ruth Neil Murry had saved many documents that provided a basis for the research, there were many gaps, particularly in the early years. Since the campus has no archives, materials were scattered in Memphis, in Knoxville and with individuals. I am grateful for the opportunities I had to talk with many former students and faculty.

Writing and production of this history would not be possible without the assistance of many people. Many alumni have shared pictures, artifacts, and memories of their student and nursing experiences. All were valuable in shaping the book, even though everything could not be included. I wish to thank the alumni and faculty who contributed specific articles at my request. I also deeply appreciate the assistance of my colleague, Dr. Cheryl Stegbauer, in her careful review and editing of each chapter. Appreciation is also expressed to Kathy Stewart, Mary Lou Wilson and Lillian Walls for their assistance. Lori Brougher provided the coordination necessary to bring the book into final production.

Our story at UT is very much like that of professional nursing in America. I hope alumni and friends will enjoy this visit into the past and reflect on what the future holds for nursing at the University of Tennessee.

E. Dianne Greenhill, EdD
Professor, UT Memphis
College of Nursing

Dedication: Tribute to Ruth Neil Murry

This 100 year history of our college is dedicated in loving memory to Miss Ruth Neil Murry, "The Dean," whose leadership spanned 40 years of this period. Miss Murry was born in Hattiesburg, Mississippi, June 26, 1913, the oldest of five children. She attended Pearl River Junior College and Mississippi Southern College.

Miss Murry became interested in nursing as a high school student when she was hospitalized for an appendectomy; however, following high school her parents wanted her to attend college rather than a school of nursing. After two-and-a-half years of college, her parents agreed for her to enroll in the University of Tennessee (UT) School of Nursing thinking the program was collegiate. Ruth Neil never told them differently. She launched her distinguished nursing career upon graduation from UT in 1936. She received the Trustees Medal from John Gaston Hospital as the member of the graduating class most attentive to the needs of patients. In 1938 she became UT's first clinical instructor in obstetric nursing after completing an eight month post-graduate course at New York Hospital, Cornell University Medical Center. Her Bachelor of Science in Nursing was awarded by UT in 1940 when the university began recognizing educational courses from other institutions as part of the nursing program. She was named educational director for the School of Nursing in 1944. In 1946 she was advanced to Director of UT School of Nursing. When the school became autonomous, Miss Murry became its first dean in 1949. Upon her retirement in December 1977, she was named emeritus dean.

circa 1960

Under Ruth Neil Murry's leadership, the school of nursing made the transition from diploma to a collegiate educational program. She expanded clinical educational opportunities and spearheaded the effort to establish the graduate program in nursing which began in 1973. She furthered her own education by earning a Master of Arts degree in nursing administration from the University of Chicago in 1953. She completed postgraduate work in higher

educational administration at Peabody College in Nashville and the UT Graduate Center in Memphis.

Miss Murry received numerous honors during her career. In 1966 she was named Memphis Professional Woman of the Year, and in 1977 she was named to Who's Who Among American Women. In 1972 she became a charter member of Beta Theta Chapter of Sigma Theta Tau International Honor Society of Nursing. The UT College of Nursing named her Outstanding Alumnus of the Year in 1974.

The Ruth Neil Murry Scholarship Fund and Ruth Neil Murry Distinguished Visiting Professorship were established in recognition of her commitment to education.

After her retirement, Miss Murry remained in close contact with the College and many of the graduates. She died Thursday, September 7, 1995, following a long illness.

(left) Ruth Neil Murry with brothers
(right) High school graduation
(center) On John Gaston Hospital steps

CHAPTER ONE

Memphis Training School for Nursing

1 8 8 7 - 1 8 9 8

The establishment of public facilities that bore any resemblance to the modern hospital did not occur in the Midsouth until the end of the nineteenth century. Prior to that time, patients who could afford to pay were cared for at home or in private infirmaries. Dr. Simon Bruech, a physician and medical historian, reported that the first public hospital in Memphis was established by an act of the Tennessee Legislature on September 20, 1829. This early hospital was built near the Mississippi River to deal with the large number of sick travelers. Residents of Memphis were not admitted.

This small inadequate hospital was replaced in 1841 with a three story brick building that was located on the site that is presently Forrest Park. After being used as a military hospital during the Civil War, the hospital was turned over to the city and became the Memphis City Hospital. That hospital was the beginning of what is now a major medical center. Most people of the 1800's considered hospitals to be unsafe and only for use by those who could not pay. Private infirmaries owned by physicians were developed for care for the more affluent. One of the first private hospitals in Memphis was the Maury and Mitchell Sanatorium for the Diseases of Women started in 1885. Drs. Richard B. Maury and Robert Wood Mitchell opened their first infirmary in a private residence at Third and Court. They built a four story building at 111 Court in 1886. This location became the site of the first training school for nurses in Tennessee and the Midsouth. Memphis Training School for Nurses was chartered September 28, 1887. The Super-

intendent of the school was Miss Winifred M. Hatch, a graduate of the Illinois Training School for Nurses.

When the Memphis Training School for Nurses opened, nursing education in the United States was still in its infancy. After the American Civil War, a few small schools of nursing began in this country. The American Civil War had demonstrated a need for trained nurses just as the Crimean War had done in Great Britain. However, it was Florence Nightingale, following her work in the Crimean, who influenced reform in hospitals in England and reformed nursing "training." Nightingale's writings began to influence nursing in this country, and the first US school based on Nightingale's principals was established in 1873 at New York's Bellevue Hospital. Two other schools, New Haven Hospital and Massachusetts General Hospital in Boston, followed later in the same year. According to historians Nutting and Dock, by 1880 there were 15 schools and 323 students in this country. This included the

Illinois Training School in Chicago developed by Miss Isabel Hampton.

The Memphis Training School for Nurses was one of the first schools of nursing in the South and certainly the first in the Midsouth. The school accepted its first student Lena Clark Angevine, in December 1887. Lena wrote that after she had been in school about six months, she enthusiastically recruited Effie Ingram of Grenada, Mississippi, to join her. Four students graduated from this 18-month program in the Spring of 1889. The other graduates were identified as Miss Dunlap of Alabama and Miss Aikens of Memphis. These three students completed the program a few months later than Lena Angevine. Lectures of three or four hours a week were given by Miss Hatch and Drs. Mitchell and Maury.

A Memphis *Commercial Appeal* (July 1, 1897) account of graduation exercises gave the following report of the school:

… the object of the school being to give a thorough course of training and theoretical instruction to young women desirous of becoming trained nurses. The course of training covers a period of eighteen months, and as soon as the nurses are far enough advanced they are sent to cases in the city upon application made by any physician who may need them. There are now in the school seven pupils. Since June 1895 there have been 148 formal applications to enter the training school, but only nineteen of this number were received on probation, ten of whom were allowed to remain as pupil nurses. It is the desire of the school to send nurses into the city to physicians who may need them, but demand has exceeded the supply of nurses, and out of 172 calls since the last report, only thirty-three nurses were supplied. The superintendent said that the young women upon whom the diplomas were to be conferred had been carefully selected with reference to the mental, moral and physical qualifications. They had also stood the test, she said, of a thorough examination upon the subjects of instruction in the school, and that now as they are sent out into the world as trained nurses the school earnestly asks for them encouragement and support… Dr. E.C. Ellett made a brief address to the graduates, pointing out to them how they should conduct themselves in the sick room. He said that they should never attempt to usurp the position of the physician, and that their profession required of them to guard carefully the secrets of families when they should be entrusted to them.

The Memphis Training School for Nurses closed in 1898 with the opening of a new city hospital and training school.

Nursing License #000001

BY E. DIANNE GREENHILL,* EdD

PROFESSOR, UT MEMPHIS COLLEGE OF NURSING

REPRINTED WITH PERMISSION FROM TENNESSEE NURSE

The contributions of Tennessee's pioneer nurse — Lena Angevine Warner — should be recognized. Yet very little was written about her during her lifetime. Lena Angevine was born in 1869 on her grandparents' plantation near Grenada, Mississippi. Her father was Saxton Angevine, a lawyer and newspaper editor. In the Grenada yellow fever epidemic of 1878, Lena reported that eight family members were "stricken," and only she and one sister survived. Angevine's early education was provided by a governess, and she then attended St. Mary's Episcopal for Girls in Memphis.

Against her family's wishes, she immediately entered the Memphis Training School for Nurses at the Maury-Mitchell Infirmary. This nursing program (chartered on December 28, 1887) was the first training school in Tennessee, and probably the Midsouth. Completing the program in 1889, Lena was the first student and first graduate nurse in Tennessee. After graduation, she went to Cook County Hospital in Chicago for a post-graduate course under Isabel Hampton. Returning to Memphis, she served as surgical assistant to Dr. R.B. Maury, a pioneer gynecologist.

Lena Angevine Warner
circa 1902

OATH

PRESCRIBED BY SECTION 1757 OF THE REVISED STATUTES OF THE UNITED STATES.
SEE ACT APPROVED MAY 13, 1884.

CITY AND COUNTY OF WASHINGTON,
DISTRICT OF COLUMBIA. } ss:

I, Mrs Lena A Warner, of Memphis, in the County of Shelby and State of Tennessee, do solemnly swear that I will support and defend the Constitution of the United States against all enemies, Foreign and Domestic; that I will bear true faith and allegiance to the same; that I take this obligation freely, without any mental reservation or purpose of evasion; and that I will well and faithfully discharge the duties of the office on which I am about to enter: So help me God.

Lena A. Warner.

Sworn and subscribed to before me this ninth day of April, 1900.

T B Hayes
Notary Public.

*Warner's U.S. Oath of Office
as a contract nurse*

Nina Wooten, one of the authors of the History of the Tennessee Nurses' Association, reports the marriage of Lena Angevine to Mr. E.C. Warner of St. Louis and of his death from a heart attack after four months of marriage. However, family members say she was divorced, a subject that was never discussed in the 1890s, Mrs. Warner again returned to work with her friend, Dr. Maury, and served as Assistant Superintendent of the Memphis Training School. In 1896, she helped organize and was president of the Memphis Trained Nurses Association, the beginning of organized nursing in Tennessee.

Lena A. Warner continued with Dr. Maury until the new Memphis City Hospital was begun around 1897. This hospital, patterned after Johns Hopkins, opened in July 1898. Mrs. Warner was involved in planning for the Hospital and became the first superintendent of

nurses. The training school at Maury-Mitchell Infirmary was transferred to the new hospital. Mrs. Warner was responsible also for leadership and instruction for the nursing school at the Memphis City Hospital, which became a part of the University of Tennessee in 1926. She is credited as the founder of the school.

The Spanish-American War (April-August 1898) brought about the need for nurses to care for the large number of troops. Diseases, including typhoid and yellow fever, caused more casualties than battles. "Trained" nurses were recruited and contracted to serve in the United States, Cuba, and the Philippines. During the war, slightly more than 1,500 nurses signed contracts with the government for military duty. The largest number on duty reached 1,158 on September 15, 1898, but was reduced to 210 by June 1899 after the typhoid epidemic subsided.

In July 1898, Lena Warner responded to an advertisement in the newspaper seeking immune nurses to serve in Cuba. After a delay due to illness with typhoid fever, Mrs. Warner signed her contact as a nurse at the salary of $50 per month beginning in April 1900. After arrival in Cuba, she was appointed Chief Nurse at the Post Hospital Matanzas, Cuba. She also served as Chief Nurse at the Columbia Barracks and later at Camp Lazear. The Army Nurse Corps (female) was established by an act of Congress on February 2, 1901, while Mrs. Warner was serving as a contract nurse. For the first time, nurses were appointed in the Regular Army. Mrs. Warner's contract was then annulled, and she was appointed to the Army Nurse Corps as Chief Nurse with the same duty.

Chief Nurse was the title used for nurses who supervised at least five other nurses. According to the *American Journal of Nursing*, there were six Army nurses on duty in Cuba in 1901. All contract nurses were offered positions as "nurse" in the Army Nurse Corps.

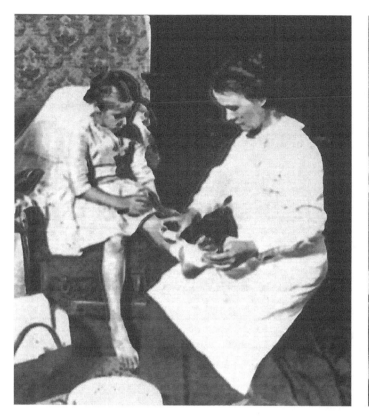 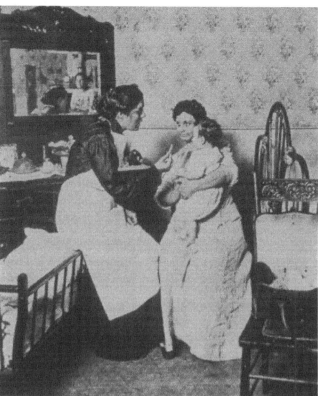

The number of nurses generally considered to be on active duty at the creation of the Corps was 220, including those at home pending discharge.

In an address to the Shelby County Medical Society in 1902, she described her experiences with yellow fever. She worked with Dr. James Carroll, Jessie Lazear, Aristide Agramoute, and Walter Reed (collectively known as the Reed Commission) in the care of yellow fever victims and research. Dr. Lazear's yellow fever research so impressed Mrs. Warner that she wrote, "I became a convert to prevention."

After a leave of absence at home, Mrs. Warner reported to the General Hospital, Presidio of San Francisco, California from May until July 1902. She was honorably discharged at her own request due to health as she "could not quite get back my health after having cholera and yellow fever on the island."

Mrs. Warner listed on her personnel record, completed in 1937 that she had a B.S. from the University of Chicago, attending between 1906-1908, but no record of any degree can be found from this university. She also studied the welfare program in Chicago. While there, she became interested in the Metropolitan Life Insurance Company's visiting nurse program. She interested the company in establishing a visiting nurse service in Memphis, which she then organized and directed for a number of years.

During the period from 1905 through 1911, Mrs. Warner devoted much of her energy to organizing nursing in Tennessee and seeking licensure for RNs. The West Tennessee Graduate Nurses' Association, an outgrowth of the earlier Memphis Trained Nurse Association, was organized with Mrs. Warner as president. Even though poorly organized, this group attempted the first statewide nursing legislation in 1905. Lack of funds prevented the bill from being presented. Mrs. Warner (in late 1905) united three separate nursing organizations —

Visiting Nurses around 1912. Photos by Coovert, courtesy of Memphis & Shelby County Health Department

Memphis, Knoxville, and Nashville — into the Tennessee State Association of Graduate Nurses and served as president until 1918. In 1907 and 1908, Mrs. Warner provided leadership for two other attempts at nursing legislation. Although both pieces of legislation were defeated, Warner noticed that nurses were becoming more politically astute.

With the support of Mayor Edward H. "Boss" Crump of Memphis, a bill was passed in February 1911, establishing a five-nurse member State Board Examiners of Nurses to be appointed by the Governor. The legislation made it unlawful "to practice professional nursing as a trained, graduate, or registered nurse" without certification. Mrs. Warner became the first Chairman of the Board and was the first licensed nurse in Tennessee. Her RN license number on file is 000001.

In 1912, the Board tried to require that RNs have a high school education and attend a nursing school in a hospital with at least 50 beds. Since only 16 of the 46 schools met this requirement, it was ignored. The leaders of small schools of nursing sponsored legislation changing the composition of the board to three physicians and two nurses and requiring schools to be under physician control. This legislation passed and was in effect until 1935. The Tennessee Nurses Association honored Mrs. Warner with a tribute and a presentation of her portrait in 1938. This portrait is currently held at TNA headquarters.

Lena Angevine Warner wearing Service Medals. Portrait presented to Tennessee Nurses Association 1938.

From 1910 to 1932, Mrs. Warner served as State chairman of the American Red Cross Nursing Department. The official history of the Red Cross recognizes her efforts in planning and assisting in organizing 20 chapters in Tennessee, as well as assisting in drives. Financed by the county chapters of the Red Cross, Public Health Nurses were placed in several counties. By November 1919, county nurses had been placed in Shelby, Maury, Knox, Blount, and Madison counties. She was awarded the American Red Cross Certificate of Merit for her distinguished service.

Mrs. Warner moved to Knoxville where she was appointed in 1916 to the position of State Health Specialist, College of Agriculture, Extension Service, University of Tennessee. She held this position until her retirement in 1946 at age 79. In this last part of her career, her activities were even more related to disease prevention in rural Tennessee and to public health. Her annual report in 1918 gives a picture of her early work.

"I have," she wrote, "on repeated visits to communities during this past year, observed here and there a sanitary privy where one had not existed before. Many homes are screened, and oil is being used to destroy mosquitos... I have observed cleaner and better ventilated homes, and this I must comment on as being most marked in the rural school rooms, demonstrating that … our visits to the rural schools have not been in vain." (Reported to Charles A. Keffer, Director, Division of Extension.)

Mrs. Warner authored several pamphlets such as "Feeding the Sick," "Typhoid: A Preventable Disease," and "Home Care of the Sick." She offered short courses on mother craft, child welfare, adolescence, and care of the sick. In 1927 she reported travel of 15,000 miles by rail and 4,823 miles by auto. At her retirement, the following summary was given of her accomplishments: "Few members of the Extension staff are more widely known or have rendered greater service to rural people of the state than Mrs. Warner. She has addressed hundreds of home demonstration and 4-H clubs and has aided thousands in achieving better health and more sanitary homes. In the early days of Extension work, she campaigned the state to arouse interest in home screening against flies. Sanitary toilets and a safer water supply for rural homes received her major attention in recent years." (*Tennessee Extension Review,* September 1946.)

The final honor she received was the unveiling of her portrait, presented by the University of Tennessee Nursing Alumni on April 12, 1948. She was ill and in a Knoxville nursing home and was unable to attend. At this time, Miss Wooten, a longtime colleague and friend, presented the biographical tribute: "I like to remember her as I last saw her — slipping in, in her unobtrusive way — to take a quiet back seat at a delegate's meeting at the State Nurse's Association convention in Knoxville. Well-built, strong figure, clear blue

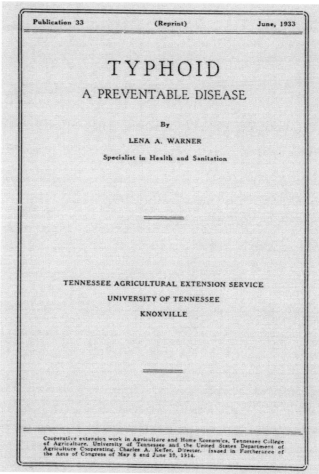

eyes, and weathered complexion, attesting her life in the open, blond hair, cut very short, plain dark suit, sensible black shoes, small black felt hat pulled down on the head with no attempt at style, spotless blouse and the little black bag that was her trademark. To see her immediately recognized — members rising all over the hall until the whole delegation was on its feet paying spontaneous tribute to her for that indomitable personality and that priceless heritage she has left to the nurses of Tennessee — the shining example." (Wooten address, Memphis, 1948)

Mrs. Warner died on August 19, 1948, and was buried in Memphis. She certainly deserves recognition as the Florence Nightingale of Tennessee. We owe to her our foundations of organized nursing, the establishment of licensure, and the provision of public health nursing throughout the state.

*E. Dianne Greenhill, a native of Tupelo, Mississippi, received a BSN from UT Memphis in 1962; an MS with majors in public health and nursing from the University of North Carolina, Chapel Hill; an EdS with majors in educational psychology and guidance from UT Knoxville; and an EdD from the University of Memphis (Memphis State) in counseling. She has served as Director of Public Health Nursing at the Memphis and Shelby County Health Department. During her 29 years as a faculty member at the UT Memphis College of Nursing, she has been Department Chair, Interim Dean and Associate Dean. Currently, she is a Professor.

CHAPTER TWO

Memphis City Hospital School of Nursing

1 8 9 8 - 1 9 2 6

No official records of the early city nursing school have been found. Elizabeth Bonner, a graduate and faculty member around 1940, wrote an unpublished paper titled "Sketch of the Development and the University of Tennessee School of Nursing" in 1942. The Bonner sketch, along with newspaper clippings, school catalogs beginning in 1926, and files of Dr. O.W. Hyman and R.N. Murry were used as the primary sources of information about this period of our history.

By levying an ad valorum tax of nine cents for the years 1895, 1896, and 1897, the City of Memphis secured the funds for purchase of a new city hospital site east of Dunlap Street at 860 Madison Avenue. The land had been an old Catholic burial ground known as St. Peter's Cemetery. On that site, construction of the new hospital began in 1897. Plans for this building were drawn to produce a small replica of Johns Hopkins Hospital. The hospital officially opened in the early summer of 1898 as the Memphis City Hospital, and the Memphis Training School became the Nursing School of the Memphis City Hospital.

The medical staff of the hospital petitioned the Mayor to appoint Mrs. Lena Angevine Warner Superintendent of Nurses at the new nursing school. She accepted the appointment and immediately began to make plans. She stated, "My one object and ambition was to give my hometown a creditable School of Nursing."

Using the Illinois Training School in

(above) Minnie Lee Nail, in Memphis City Hospital Training School uniform, 1906
(right) Memphis City Hospital completed 1898

Chicago as a basis, Mrs. Warner set up the two-year nursing curriculum that included a one-month probationary period upon entry. Requirements for admission included a letter from the family physician stating the physical condition of the applicant, a letter from the pastor of her church stating her moral character, and an educational background of high school or its equivalent. Many of the applicants came from public schools of that day, which were inferior to private or Church schools.

Uniforms were dark blue with a full, white apron gathered onto a band. A very small white cap was pinned on the top of the head. Students wore no jewelry except a plain watch on a black cord around the neck.

Student hours on duty were from 7 a.m. to 7 p.m., with two hours off duty, and one afternoon free each week. Additionally, students alternated duty one-half day every other Sunday. Two students at a time were on night duty with Miss Thompson, who was Mrs. Warner's only assistant and also night supervisor. There were 10 students at this time, and a patient bed capacity of 100.

Students' living quarters were on the second floor of the three-story hospital building with a large room on the first floor in which to entertain friends in the evening. On one evening each week students were allowed to either entertain friends at the hospital or with special permission, be out in the city visiting until 10 p.m.

A medical staff was appointed whose political prestige largely influenced their selection. By 1899 the medical staff were well organized and were included in the teaching program as lecturers to the student nurses. (See the following charts for the curriculum.)

Classes also met once each week for practical demonstrations in nursing, ethics, and recitations. Every three months a written review was given. Text books included: Isabel Hampton's *Practice of Nursing*, Potter's *Materia Medica*, and Gray's *Anatomy*.

During the second year, students worked in the Operating Room where they were taught Surgical Technic (sic), names of instruments, precautions in sterilizing, care of sponges, and bandages and their uses.

Mrs. Warner was the only instructor. Dr. Pope Farrington was the "physician-in-charge." Mrs. Warner stayed with the school for only 15 months; late in 1899, she volunteered for service in the care of yellow fever victims following the Spanish-American War.

The school was chartered in 1900, and the eight members of the first graduating class received diplomas from the Memphis City Hospital Training School of Nurses. They proudly wore the large gold hospital pin. This class included Miss Lula K. Robley, who, until the time of her death, was closely associated with the Alumnae Association founded by Mrs. Warner.

Miss Nell A. (Nellie) Peeler reported in

1899 – First Year

Anatomy, *6 lectures*	Dr. Laus
Physiology, *12 lectures*	Dr. Black
Obstetrics, *8 lectures*	Dr. W.W. Taylor
Materia Medica & Physiologic Action of Drugs, *8 lectures*	Dr. Erskine

Second Year

Physiology & Organic Functions *12 lectures*	Dr. Black
Obstetrics, *12 lectures*	Dr. W.W. Taylor
Asepsis & Surgical Cleanliness *4 lectures*	Dr. J.M. Maury
Materia Medica, *4 lectures*	Dr. Erskine

(left) 1900 graduate Lula K. Robley in later years.
(below) Class of 1903 graduation, photo by Coovert

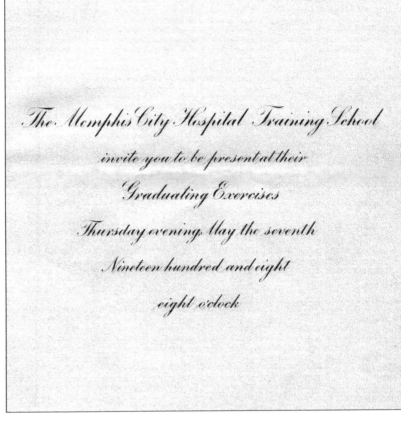

The Memphis City Hospital Training School

invite you to be present at their

Graduating Exercises

Thursday evening, May the seventh

Nineteen hundred and eight

eight o'clock

(top) Memphis City Hospital Training School students and faculty 1906 (bottom) Nursing students with nursing superintendent and physicians, circa 1907 (right) 1908 graduation invitation

January 1908 City Hospital Annual Report that she accepted the position of Superintendent of Nurses on July 13, 1907, after having been in charge of the operating room since 1905. "The school consisted of a class of fourteen pupil nurses (a class of seven having just been graduated the preceding June). Upon recommendation of the Hospital Staff, the Trustees increased the number of nurses from fourteen to eighteen. We now have a corps of eighteen pupil nurses and a graduate nurse in charge of the operating room. This increase of nurses enables us to give the proper and necessary attention, both day and night, to all patients — charity or pay. I am also able to give special nurses to private patients, when the wards are not so heavy as to need the entire corps. Of the eighteen nurses now in the school, four are seniors and fourteen juniors…"

The May 1908 graduation of four seniors

held in the operating room of the hospital was reported in *The Commercial Appeal.* "The operating room in which they graduated was tastefully decorated with the class colors, blue and white, while a background of palms and potted plants relieved the severity of the white tiled walls. Immediately behind the class were seated the staff of pupil nurses … The graduates were garbed in white and were ushered into the room by Miss Nellie Peeler, the head nurse, under whose direction they have been for the past year. Rising high above the floor of the operating room were the tiers of seats used week days by students of the two medical colleges, and filled last night almost to overflowing."

The course of training completed by these graduates was described as "two years work in all of the various wards, private rooms and operating room in the hospital. Members of the hospital staff, selected by the school committee,

deliver a series of lectures, three each week for six months in the year. It is upon the lines of these lectures and their practical work that the nurses are examined."

In 1911 the Memphis City Hospital had five interns, 15 student nurses, a superintendent of nurses who was also an instructor, one assistant, and a graduate nurse in charge of the operating room. Students often were sent to the police station to care for ill prisoners. Student living quarters were still on the second floor of the hospital, but in 1912 the city purchased the old Seldon home. It was a two-story, frame residence that adjoined the hospital grounds. The home accommodated 60 student nurses after a three-story brick addition in 1916. Mrs. Julia Funk, who was born in Alsace-Lorraine and came to Memphis in 1890, became matron of this residence. For 23 years, she was a substitute mother for her girls.

In 1912 an old workshop next door to the morgue in the rear of the hospital grounds was enlarged and used for a contagion hospital. It contained about 20 beds for patients, a room for the nurse in charge, and a room for a maid who lived at the hospital, a small combined kitchen and dining room, and a medicine room. Dr. Percy Wood was the first visiting or staff doctor. One student nurse was on 24-hour duty unless patients required nursing care at night. In that case, both a day and a night nurse were on straight 12 hour duty. Nurses were not allowed to leave the building at any time, nor were visitors allowed. Nurses usually spent from four to eight weeks in this service, during which time they were in complete isolation. Behind this building was a pasture for sheep that were used by the medical college for experimental purposes.

Graduates of 1908 with Miss Peeler. Photo courtesy of Robert Skinner and family

*T*he following article about the Memphis City Hospital was written by John L. Tait and appeared in *The Commercial Appeal* August 18, 1912. The article provides a vivid description of the hospital and students at that time:

The Memphis City Hospital, which has so often been a bone of contention in political and medical circles, appears to have fairly settled down, for the time being at least, to the achievement to its normal destiny. Some changes have been made. Some new features added. Some reforms introduced.

Note, the distinction — changes, new features, reforms, for they are not synonymous, although sometimes they overlap in practical effects.

Perhaps the most important new feature is the nurses' home. This is a substantial frame building adjoining the hospital grounds in which the pupil nurses of the institution, and all others for that matter, have a local habitation.

The building is presided over by a matron, who works under the rules of the superintendent and is directly amenable to him. She is vested with immediate control of the home, and with immediate authority over the conduct of its inmates. If there lurks anywhere a haunting suspicion that her job is a sinecure, it is in the bosom of somebody who doesn't know.

The pupil nurses are a nice lot of girls — as nice as any thirty girls you can scare up in a day's ride anywhere; but you take that number of them, with all their inevitable variety of disposition and temperament and irrepressible frolicsomeness upon occasion, and try to hold them within the purview of any set of rules on earth — and you will be an applicant within a month for a cot in the neurasthenic ward.

The matron managed by treating them as a lot of children. By a little fiction which nobody has ever put into print before, and which everybody outwardly ignores by common consent while tacitly recognizing it in his heart, the matron is mother or stepmother, or mother-in-law as occasion and individual demands, to the whole bevy of them.

This isn't saying that there is a single objectionable girl in the lot. It is merely stating, what everybody knows to be true, although one would never believe it seeing them only on duty or at church, that pupil nurses are as human as other folks, and like a laugh, and occasionally a good cry, and are subject to personal likes and dislikes and whims the same as girls uninformed.

A Home of Their Own

The home is a big thing for the nurses. Heretofore they have been obliged to room in the hospital building. Something like a dozen of them must do so still, for that matter.

It is necessary to have some of them close at hand in case of an emergency call from the wards. But the bulk of them have now a place which they regard with justifiable pride and affection as home — a place which gives them rest and more of the rest and detachment from professional life which are so dear to femininity than they could even have secured under the cold conditions, within the hospital building itself.

It is a good thing for the hospital. It gives the institution a corps of nurses who are better rested and refreshed and capable of better service than used to be the case. It makes for discipline within the institution. A bacteriological and pathological department has been added.

This was one of the crying needs of the hospital, and has already repaid manifold the expense of its installation. It is in charge of Dr. Jesse J. Cullings, one of the best equipped pathologists of the South, and is already regarded as an indispensable adjunct to the hospital service.

Formerly all the work now done in this department had to be taken down town to the city bacteriologist or to some pathological expert, who required a fee for services rendered. Now, in addition to the lessening of expense, the work is done on the spot with an expedition hitherto impossible.

Memphis City Hospital

The Receiving Wards

Two receiving wards have been added. Heretofore there has been none at all.

Heretofore when a patient came to then hospital he was carried immediately to one of the wards, or if a surgical case indicating immediate attention, into the operation room. Patients coming into the institution in the middle of the night, and carried upstairs into wards full of sleeping patients, introduce more or less confusion and disturb the patients in the wards.

Now they are taken into one of the receiving wards, which are fully equipped for minor surgical operations, as well as prepared for the temporary accommodation of the patients. If in need of minor operations, they can be attended to without removal to the regular operating room. If not, they can at least be retained in the receiving wards until hours suitable for their transfer to the regular wards of the hospital…

Can Take Care of 190

The Memphis city hospital as it stands today has a capacity of about 190 patients. That it was none too large is evident from the fact that on the day of the visitation there

(left) Nurses Residence 1912-1927
(right) Graduating Class 1912.
Photo by Coovert

were in the various wards 160 patients. The average number of patients during the month of June was 135. During the month of July it was slightly more. August, thus far, shows a decided increase.

The doors of the institution stand wide to all the sick and injured. "First aid to all the world" might very properly be written across lintels. But there is a certain discrimination exercised once first aid has been rendered.

When a call is sent in for an ambulance, the ambulance surgeon hustles aboard the vehicle and is hiked to the clangor of gong and the chugging of the gasoline motor, across town to the side of the patient. Here a superficial examination is made, to determine the nature and extent of the aid required. If possible, this is administered on the spot. Otherwise the injured party is bundled into the ambulance, and the hurry run for the hospital begins.

Rules of Admission

This is all true, whether the patient is a resident of Memphis or hails from beyond the seven seas. But in case of one who is simply sick and applies for admission and treatment—one who does not require "first aid"—the officials of the hospital first inquire his residence. If he lives in Memphis, he is at once taken in and assigned his proper place in a ward. But if he lives out of the city, he is refused admission except as a pay patient. Otherwise the institution would be unable to supply the demands upon it.

There are quite a number of Memphis patients who voluntarily become pay patients rather than accept the charity of the city. These are charged $1.50 a day. Out of town patients pay $2 a day. For this sum they are provided with room and board, ordinary medicine, and the service of the house staff

and pupil nurses. Those who desire it may employ their own physicians and graduate nurses at their own expense.

It costs money to run an institution like this. It costs from $5,000 to $6,000 and up per month. It is costing less just now than it has in the past, owing to some of the changes and reforms enforced.

One of the needs of the hospital is another ambulance. This has already been ordered, and will shortly be in service. It is to be an Anderson electric car with a wheel base of 100 inches, specifically arranged for extra easy riding and furnished with stretcher and all other standard ambulance equipment.

The hospital is managed by the following staff, Charles R. Mason, superintendent; Miss Frances E. Spences, superintendent of nurses; Miss J. Pabor, head operating nurse; Sam Wharton, chief clerk; J.F. Ward, accountant; Elinio Courley, apothecary; Tom Williams, steward; and J.F. Walden, chief engineer.

The following are the interns: Drs. T.N. Coppedge (ambulance surgeon); J.T. Raynor, T. Parmelee, F.G. Jones, P.R. Cruse, R.B. Alley, Floyd Webb and J. R. Crawford.

The operators assigned for the summer term are the following: Surgery, Dr. McCowan and Dr. Braum; medicine, Dr. McMann and Dr. Pistole; gynecology, Dr. Graham; obstetrics, Dr. Price and Dr. Bridger; eye, Dr. Price; throat, Dr. Lewis; dermatology, Dr. Hanse; neurology, Dr. Somerville; and orthopedics, Dr. Campbell.

The hospital operates under the board of trustees. These officials have delegated the immediate supervision of the institution of the superintendent. The present board of trustees is composed of R.O. Johnston, chairman; M.M. Bosworth and St. Elmo Newton.

(above) Snapshots of Memphis General Hospital nursing students, interns and patients, circa 1918

In 1913 the hospital became the teaching center of the College of Medicine of the University of Tennessee, and Miss Evelyn Stevenson (Ward), a graduate of St. Luke's Hospital in Chicago, was appointed Superintendent of Nurses. She increased the two-year program to three years and instituted an intensive course in theory. The first three-year class had six members and graduated May 27, 1915. At that time, there were 46 students in the school. An elective course in Operating Room Technic (sic) was offered to students in their senior year if they seemed "fitted" for this service, and the students' preliminary period was lengthened to six months. Mrs. Evelyn Stevenson Ward added a full time instructor to the staff, Miss Clara Schuhardt, who was a graduate of St. Luke's Hospital.

Mrs. Ward was made an honorary member of the Alumnae Association in recognition of her outstanding service in the development of the school. She took an active part in promoting better legislation for nurses, in Red Cross activities, and taught classes in Home Hygiene. In 1918 during World War I, Mrs. Ward, along with two graduates nurses, four student nurses, and a large number of volunteer workers, took charge of the nursing service of the Red Cross Hospital that was located in Central High School. Mrs. Ward resigned from the nursing school on December 31, 1920, to accept a position as chief laboratory technician with The University of Tennessee.

The uniform dress for students was changed in 1914 from dark blue to light blue

1916 Curriculum

A hospital experience called "Headnurseship" was given during the third year. In addition to their work in the hospital, students received planned instruction that was described by Bonner as follows:

Preliminary Course — 1ST SIX MONTHS

During this course, the members of the class spent 2 hours a day in practical work on the wards, 3 hours in study and 3 hours in lecture and demonstration, except for one-half day free on Saturday and Sunday.

SUBJECTS:

Practical Nursing	Theoretical Nursing
Ethics	Anatomy
Materia Medica	Bacteriology
Chemistry	

Junior Class — 2ND SIX MONTHS OF THE FIRST YEAR

Anatomy and Physiology	12 hours
Materia Medica	12 hours
Hygiene and Sanitation	8 hours
Bacteriology	8 hours
Prophylaxis	6 hours

Intermediate Class — SECOND YEAR

Anatomy and Physiology	24 hours
Materia Medica	12 hours
Minor Surgery and Surgical Technic	12 hours
Dietetics	16 hours
Bacteriology	12 hours
Medicine	12 hours
Gynecology	8 hours

Senior Class — THIRD YEAR

Review of Anatomy and Physiology	8 hours
Review of Materia Medica	8 hours
Pediatrics	12 hours
Massage	18 hours
Neurology	6 hours
Ophthalmology	8 hours
Obstetrics	12 hours
Ear, Eye, Nose & Throat	8 hours
Contagious Diseases and Dermatology	8 hours
History of Nursing	8 hours
American Journal of Nursing	12 hours

with white stripes. The aprons worn were still full and gathered on a band with bibs crossing in the back. The cap remained the same. In 1915 the hospital pin was changed to a somewhat smaller one with a blue cross, with the hospital color, surrounded by a circle of yellow gold.

Mr. Jeptha F. Ward was appointed Superintendent of the Hospital in 1915, and except for a short time in 1920-21, served until his death in 1943. He recognized the hospital's future possibilities as a medical center, and it is largely due to his effort that the tremendous additions of the next decade took place.

In 1914 a one-story children's pavilion was built with a 20-bed capacity. The number of graduate registered nurses on the staff was eight. There were 16 students in training at this time, and each student averaged 54 hours per week on duty. In 1916 the name of the hospital was changed to Memphis General Hospital, and in 1918 the bed capacity was increased to 239.

Around 1916 there was still only one full-time nurse instructor. Student curriculum and hospital assignments for the three-year period are shown above and on page 21. During the years 1918-1920, the hours of study decreased and standards declined due to World War I. However, many of the graduates volunteered their services in the war through the Red Cross. Two units were sent from Memphis.

Base Hospital 57, entirely a Memphis Unit and the first to be made up entirely in one city, was headed by Dr. Frank Smythe, Sr., and Dr. E.C. Mitchell, chosen because of his West Point experience. City hospital nursing graduates were Miss Elizabeth Dabney, Miss Ivy Tommie Thum, Miss Cynthia Chism (Mrs. Richards), Miss Edna Roach (Mrs. Campbell), Miss Helen Struble (Mrs. Fred Fiedler), Miss Alberta Robinson, Miss Laura Lewis, Miss Gardner (Mrs. Rogers), and Miss Ruth Beatty.

Unit P, organized and commanded by Dr. Battle Malone, was headed by Miss Myrtle Archer, a 1907 graduate of this School. This group, who left Memphis in 1917, was the first unit from the Southern United States to go to France. The unit was stationed at Chaumont, Haute Marne, American Headquarters in France and later assigned to Base Hospital 15. From there, groups of nurses were sent to various points near the front line.

Besides Miss Archer, other graduates of the school in Unit P were Miss Mattie L. Shaffer (Mrs. Edwards), Miss Annie Colquitt, Miss Jean Hope (Mrs. Meil), Miss Mildred Durr (Mrs. R.B. McCormick), Miss Myrtle Bishop, and Miss Etta Williamson (Mrs. Culverhouse).

In 1921 a laboratory building was erected at the expense of the University. In 1922 a segregated 60-bed Isolation Hospital was built to care for contagious diseases of all kinds.

In 1920 the Memphis General Hospital became a university hospital when, by contractual agreement, The University of Tennessee College of Medicine accepted responsibility for the medical care of the patients. From 1921 to 1923, there were six or seven Directors of Nursing, who each remained only a few months. Changes began in the nursing school when Miss Winifred W. Atkinson was appointed Superin-

1916 Student Hospital Assignments

General Medicine	4 months Male and 4 months Female
General Surgery	4 months Male and 4 months Female
Children	1 month
Diets	1 month
Obstetrics	4 months, no. of deliveries required to be seen: 24
Operating Room	4 months
Orthopedics	1 month
Contagion	1 month
Night Duty	6 months
Vacation	2 months

Nervous and Mental Diseases and Tuberculosis – only odd cases

tendent of Nurses in September 1923. Miss Atkinson, graduate of London Hospital in London, England, had been in education and administration in the United States for 20 years. As superintendent, her goal was to have the school approved by the New York Board of Regents (Bonner, 1942; *The Commercial Appeal*, July 24, 1926). Approval by this group allowed graduates of a program to obtain licensure by endorsement in the state of New York. Miss Doty, a representative of the University of New York State Department of Education Board of Nurse Examiners, visited the school on March 31, 1924. Efforts were made to upgrade the curriculum and raise standards. No record of the results of the approval process has been found.

Mrs. Earl A. Harris, an untiring supporter of the school, was made a member of the hospital's Board of Trustees in 1924. She was the first woman Board member, a position she held for many years. In a historical sketch (Bonner, 1942), it was noted that during all her years of service, Mrs. Harris had taken a deep interest in the students and had done a great deal toward promoting beneficial cultural opportunities for them.

Nursing education provided at Memphis General Hospital was similar to that in other hospital training schools in the 1920's. There was an apprenticeship system of education with the school existing primarily to provide students to care for patients in hospitals. The Goldmark report published in 1923, pointed out the problems in hospital training schools and

Nurse in World War I uniform

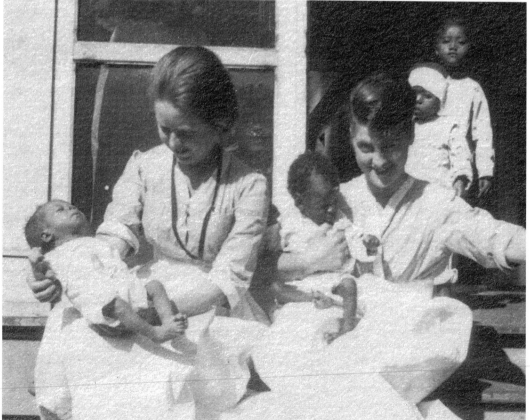

*Snapshots from Memphis
General Hospital 1919-1920.
Photos courtesy of Doris
Rudisill Stern, Class of 1922*

(left) Snapshot from Memphis General Hospital 1919-1920. Photo courtesy of Doris Rudisill Stern, Class of 1922 (right) Graduating class of 1922

the need to establish schools of nursing in universities for nursing leadership (Kalisch & Kalisch, 1986). The American Nurses' Association surveyed the approximately 2100 schools of nursing in 1925. Only 224 out of the 1,500 that responded had a minimum entrance requirement of four years of high school. Also, 440 schools had a student body of 19 or fewer students. Many of the hospitals where the schools were centered had a daily patient census of less than 50. (Kalisch & Kalisch, 1986).

"The School of Nursing has been launched on a University basis" (*The Univ. of TN Record*, Nov. 1926, p. 19). This important event was the result of several years of effort by Miss Winifred Atkinson, Superintendent of Nurses, and Mrs. Earl Harris, a member of the board of directors of the Memphis General Hospital. The Board of Trustees of the Hospital met with the UT Dean of Administration, Dr. O.W. Hyman, on July 22, 1926, and agreed on a contract creating the University of Tennessee

School of Nursing. The City of Memphis and the University of Tennessee on November 9, 1926, entered into a contract governing the operation of the Memphis General Hospital by the College of Medicine.

This 50-year contract stated: "…the University of Tennessee will incorporate the School of Nurses into its College of Medicine as a department of instruction and will… provide a teaching staff and other facilities sufficient to maintain the School in the highest class established by recognized standardizing agencies, and that the teaching staff of the School of Nurses shall be confirmed both by the Board of Trustees of the University of Tennessee and by the Board of Trustees of the Memphis General Hospital before appointment and that any member of the staff may be discharged only with the consent of both said boards of trustees. Space, equipment and supplies for the courses in the scientific subjects such as Anatomy, Physiology, Bacteriology,

(continued on page 27)

(top) Nursing faculty and students,
circa 1924 or 25
(center left) Faculty and Students of
Memphis General Hospital School
for Nurses 1923. Miss Winifred
Atkinson, Director, (front row
center), Miss Hinton, Assistant,
(front row right)
(center right) Graduating class,
circa 1925
(bottom) Memphis General Hospital
nurses on duty August 1, 1925

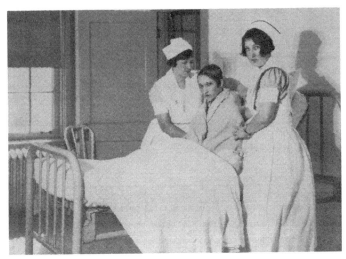

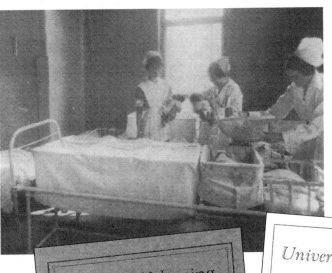

School of Nursing

of the

Memphis General Hospital

Memphis, Tennessee

*Affiliated with the
Medical Department of the
University of Tennessee*

The
University of Tennessee
Memphis
SCHOOL OF NURSING

MEMPHIS GENERAL HOSPITAL

THE UNIVERSITY OF TENNESSEE, in conjunction with the Memphis General Hospital, offers a course of training leading to the degree of Graduate in Nursing in three years. The School of Nursing, as a department of the State University, is in the forefront of American schools. The Memphis General Hospital with three hundred and fifty beds for both acute infections, diseases and chronic cases offers ideal material for a well-rounded training, while the scientific laboratories, equipment, and staff of the class A College of Medicine of the University provide the most thorough scientific preparation for the hospital training.

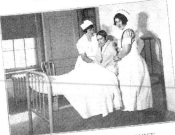

School of Nursing

DEMAND FOR NURSING SERVICE

THE public demand for nursing service increases steadily as living standards improve and hospitalization becomes more widespread. Except in times of great wars, there has never before been such a demand for well-trained nurses as now exists in our country. Increasing numbers of nurses are needed for public health nursing, school nursing service, and maternity nursing.

The Department of Public Health of the State of Tennessee is in need of a considerable number of nurses now and the educative aspect of this type of nursing service appeals to many.

Public schools use graduate nurses in protecting the health of school children, especially in detecting defects of the eyes, ears, and teeth that may be referred to physicians or dentists for treatment.

(left) 1926 School of Nursing bulletin
(above) UT School of Nursing, circa 1927

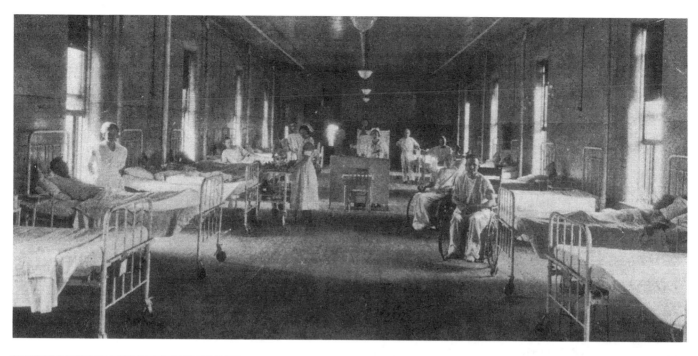

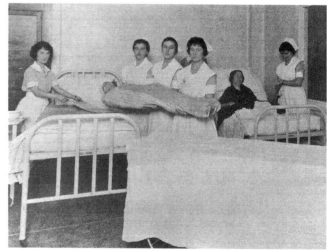

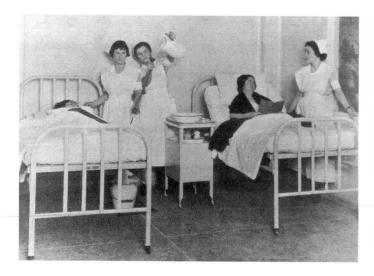

(top) Memphis General Hospital Ward, circa 1925
(center left) Efficiency Record of Nursing Student: Part of Final Transcript of Memphis General Hospital Graduates in 1920's
(center right) A Practical Nursing Procedure
(left) Practical Course in Nursing
(right, pictured l-r) Miss Emma Sydleman, RN Instructress, student, and Miss Winfred Atkinson

1926 Curriculum

First Year

FIRST SEMESTER

Nursing Procedures	96 hours
Principles of Nursing	32 hours
Anatomy & Physiology	40 hours
Bacteriology	30 hours
Bandaging	12 hours
Solutions & Elem Materia Medica	24 hours
Hygiene & Sanitation	10 hours
Chemistry	32 hours
Nutrition & Cooking	40 hours
History of Nursing	10 hours
Nursing Ethics	16 hours

SECOND SEMESTER

Materia Medica	36 hours
Diet Therapy	16 hours
Anatomy & Physiology	40 hours
Elements of Pathology	16 hours

Second Year

FIRST SEMESTER

Surgical Nursing	24 hours
Surgical Techinique	10 hours
Medical Nursing	20 hours
Obstetrics	18 hours
Gynecology	10 hours

SECOND SEMESTER

Diseases of Children	36 hours
Otology	8 hours
Ophthalmology	8 hours
Orthopedics	8 hours

Third Year

FIRST SEMESTER

Massage	10 hours
Dermatology & VD	8 hours
Nervous & Mental	8 hours
Advanced Nursing Procedures	10 hours

SECOND SEMESTER

Psychology	16 hours
Problems of Priv Duty	2 hours
Economic & Soc Prob	6 hours
Public Health & TB	4 hours
Parliamentary Law	4 hours
Review	10 hours

*Patient in front of hospital
circa 1925*

Chemistry, Materia Medica, and Pathology for the School of Nursing shall be furnished by the University of Tennessee, but space, equipment and supplies for the courses in the practical nursing subjects such as Nursing Procedures, Bandaging, Medical Nursing, and Surgical Nursing shall be furnished by the General Hospital." (*Univ. of TN Board of Trustees Minutes*, Vol 10, pp 194-206.)

The first bulletin or catalog of the school of nursing published in 1926 lists the admission requirements and curriculum. In 1926 two years of high school work or its equivalent were considered minimum for admission. The young woman was to be between 18 and 35 years of age, to be of average weight, height, physique,

and in good physical condition. The courses of instruction are shown in the chart above.

The Principal of the School of Nursing was listed as Winifred W. Atkinson; however she died on July 23, 1926. Her death occurred shortly after the University and hospital merger of the school was approved, a goal for which she had worked for years. Ella George Hinton, who was a graduate of the 1917 class of the Memphis General Hospital, was Assistant to the Principal in 1926. Miss Hinton became Superintendent of Nurses upon Miss Atkinson's death and served as acting director of the school until 1945. The bulletin also listed 20 faculty members, 15 with titles of ward supervisor. Most of the subjects were taught by physicians.

CHAPTER THREE

The University of Tennessee and Growth of the Diploma Program 1926-1950

The University began operation of the School of Nursing in June 1927. The first official University of Tennessee School of Nursing Bulletin was published April 1927. In that publication, the curriculum and calendar were based on the quarter system in keeping with the other schools on campus. Instructors in nursing included Miss Laura Odell, who was in charge of the school, and Mrs. Lucenda Smith. Requirements for admission were revised to include four years of high school or 15 credits with specific course requirements listed.

"After the successful completion of the preliminary period of training, the student enters upon a graduated ward service of nine quarters. Two quarters are spent on the medical wards, two on the surgical wards, one on communicable diseases, one on pediatrics, one on obstetrics, and one in the out-patient department. The final quarter is given to public health nursing. The didactic courses of the curriculum after the preliminary period are strictly correlated with the ward nursing service." (*Bulletin*, 1927, p.16).

The year 1927 was also noteworthy for the school in that a new nurses' residence with classroom space was opened and dedicated on January 7. The three-story building was located on the east side of the hospital grounds and named for Dr. Marcus Haase. In addition to two classrooms, it had quarters for 125 nurses, Miss Hinton and Miss Julia Funk, who was matron of the home. Nursing students were housed in this facility until the 1960's.

The UT Board of Trustees report in 1928 noted the enrollment in the School of Nursing was 82 in 1927 and 88 in 1928. The desire was to increase this number to 160. "One of the most pressing needs… instruction and administration in schools of nursing. The University is seeking to meet this need by offering a

Marcus Haase Nurses' Residence, 1926

1927 students pose in front of Marcus Haase Nurses' residence

combined course in the College of Liberal Arts and the School of Nursing for women of exceptional promise. The course entitles one to the degrees of Bachelor of Science and Graduate in Nursing at the end of the five-year curriculum." (*Univ. of TN Record,* Nov. 1928, p. 42). For many years few students completed this option.

Once the School of Nursing was established as a part of the University, recruiting efforts to find a director were initiated. Miss Ella George Hinton was listed as "acting" director because of her lack of academic qualifications. Dr. O.W. Hyman was administrative officer for the campus. He wrote to nursing leaders in the country asking for nominations to fill the position of Director of the School of Nursing of The University of Tennessee and Superintendent of Nurses of the Memphis General Hospital. The salary in March 1928 was listed as "$2400 to $3000 annually and

maintenance consisting of the use of a private suite of rooms in the new nurses' home, board and laundry." The staff of the school to support the director was listed "as one (or two) assistant directors, one night supervisor, three instructors, one assistant instructor, eleven departmental supervisors, and a secretary." As was true in many nursing programs of the period, little or no distinction was made between hospital nursing staff and instructional staff.

A response out of Yale University School of Nursing contained interesting observations about the hospital and university relationship. "I am wondering with the title by which you are describing the director of the school, whether or not she is to have faculty rank and just what will be the relationship of the school to the university. This does not appear to me to be very clear. Do I understand also that the school is to form the nursing service of the hospital upon which it will wholly depend? ... if the school is to be a university school of nursing it might be possible someone might be interested in accepting the position..." (letter to O.W. Hyman, April 28, 1928). No one was ever recruited or hired for the described position.

In 1931 Dr. Hyman attempted to design an educational program for a student in School of Nursing who already had a baccalaureate degree and who would work toward the master's degree in preparation to assume the directorship of the school. He corresponded with the University of Minnesota and Teacher's College. In a letter of May 20, 1931 to Elizabeth Burgess of Teacher's College, Dr. Hyman stated the leadership problem of the school: "We feel that we are handicapped at present in the improvement of our school by the fact that the Director of the School, who is also Superintendent of Nurses in the Memphis General Hospital has only a high school education and received her training in a nursing school that was poorly organized. She is a woman of character, but she feels her inadequacy to such a degree that she will not assume responsibility for any instruction and is loathe to initiate any changes in the current routine of hospital administration as it affects the nursing service."

These plans to "grow" a director from within the school did not materialize.

In the late 20's and early 30's, the University employed only two nursing faculty who were primarily responsible for instruction. Other nurses identified as faculty were supervisors and staff of the Memphis General Hospital. By 1929 Mrs. Lucenda Smith had resigned as faculty and was replaced by Miss Bernice Rankin, a graduate of Cincinnati General Hospital. Miss Terry Brady replaced Miss Rankin in February 1934. In September 1934, Miss Katherine Upchurch, who had a non-nursing baccalaureate and master's from The University of Tennessee, Knoxville and graduated from Yale University School of Nursing, was employed as theoretical instructor. According to Ruth Neil Murry, who was a student during this period, Miss Upchurch was identified as the educational director of the program. The first nursing faculty member to carry the formal title of Educational Director was Miss Frances H. Cunningham, a B.S. graduate of Kansas State College and nursing graduate of Charlotte Swift Memorial Hospital, Manhattan, N.Y. Miss Upchurch apparently left the school around 1936 and was replaced by Miss Cunningham. The leadership acutely needed by the school was provided by Miss Cunningham until February 1, 1944, when she resigned to return to Western Reserve University to complete her master's degree. Effective July 1, 1935 the University and Memphis General Hospital entered into an agreement that ten additional instructors in the School of Nursing would be employed. The hospital was to provide board and laundry, and the university was to provide salaries.

The Committee on the Grading of Nursing Schools began work in 1928-29 with the purpose of improving quality of nursing, increasing quantity, and lowering cost to the patient. Unemployment of nurses was a problem of the Depression period, but the report of the Committee on Grading noted that the large numbers of unemployed graduates were due to the large number of schools. The summary published in 1934 reported half of all nursing schools in the U.S. were connected with hospitals having 75 patients or less and that the typical school had only 43 students. By 1929 only 73 percent of students had finished high school. By 1930 entrance requirements for the school of nursing at UT were standardized to be the same as those entering the College of Liberal Arts at Knoxville. The enrollment had increased to about 150 students total, 20 per entering section (*Univ. of TN Record*, November 1930).

The 1930 UT Bulletin listed for the first time a two-quarter postgraduate course in Anesthesia. The Biennial Report for 1930 stated: "There is also need of more nurses trained to act as anesthetists, x-ray technicians, laboratory technicians, or public health nurses. A postgraduate course in anesthesia will be offered for the first time in 1931..." The course in anesthesia admitted four nurses at the beginning of each quarter. School records do not indicate how long the anesthesia program continued.

Miss Frances Cunningham, Educational Director, UT School of Nursing 1936-1944

The John Gaston Hospital, completed in 1936

The 1932 Biannual Report for the Health Division at Memphis noted the cost of instructing students for the school year 1931-1932 was $18,961.01. Total enrollment was reported as 200, so cost per student was given as $81.49. Enrollment for 1932-33 was listed as 222. An increase in the number of applicants was a significant change for the school. Only 100 students from an applicant pool of 400 could be admitted. The serious problem of overcrowding the profession was a concern. Dr. Hyman wrote expressing the need for emphasis on education for nurses as opposed to labor for hospitals. "It seems obvious that some relief must soon be given the nursing profession in the form of legislative enactments that will lessen the exploitation of young women in providing cheap labor for hospitals. We should provide additional teaching personnel as soon as our budget permits. We still require too much labor of the student and provide too little educational opportunity."

In July 1934, Dr. Hyman wrote a letter to Acting University President Dr. James D.

Hoskins and presented a program of development for the next five years. Goals for the School of Nursing were: "Development of School of Nursing as an educational institution and its divorce from financial entanglement with the hospital should be pushed along. It will be necessary to employ an intelligent and highly trained director to give full time to the undertaking before much progress can be expected."

Also in the 1934 Biannual Report the following statement appears: "The University plans to encourage the hospital to remove some of its labor requirements from the pupil nurse and thus free her energies for a more thoroughgoing course of training in both the fundamental and applied aspects of nursing. In other words, the University will continue to emphasize the educational aspects of the nurse's training. Enrollment in the School of Nursing will not be increased but the educational opportunities of the pupil nurse will be improved."

The School of Nursing had a new clinical home when the main building of the Memphis General Hospital was demolished in 1934 to make room for the new John Gaston Hospital that was dedicated on June 27, 1936. The new hospital contained 600 beds. Most of the faculty had offices on the wards while classes continued to be held in Marcus Haase and the Anatomy, Pharmacy, and Pathological Institute buildings.

Improvement of the educational program continued as a goal of the University; however, the hospital continued to require students to provide a large part of the nursing care. Miss Cunningham in 1938-39 sent objectives to Dr. Hyman stating the two main objectives of improving the quality of teaching both in the classroom and wards and improving the quality of nursing care for the hospital. Plans for the year included an educational program for supervisors and head nurses. Two courses were to be taught by Miss Phoebe Kandel from the extension division of Colorado State College of Education: "Ward Management and Ward

Capping Ceremony in 1939. Faculty (in white uniforms) on front row – Miss Dukes, Miss Hinton, Miss Cunningham

Teaching" and "The Curriculum and Methods of Teaching Applied to Nursing" to be offered for college credit. Also, Miss Cunningham noted that each hospital nursing service should be staffed adequately to prevent student nurses from being transferred from one service to another to meet the nursing service needs.

During 1938-39 the ward teaching program was expanded to include morning reports for 15 to 30 minutes on three to six days a week to aid the students in correlating classroom theory with patients on the wards. The course in Public Health Nursing was increased from 11 to 22 hours. Drs. Frank Roberts and Henry Packer assisted in teaching this course. Each student was assigned one day to visit with a city health department nurse.

As of January 1939, there were 150 students in the nursing program. Concerns expressed by Miss Cunningham included the very limited extra-curricular activities of the students and conditions in the nurses' residence. "The atmosphere of the home is in no way conducive

to study." She recommended someone be employed to be on duty in the home from 4 p.m. to midnight to ensure that all students were in the home, that they go to bed at a reasonable hour, and to keep the home quiet for those who wish to sleep or study. This "hostess" also was to know what type of company the nurses keep and in what condition they come home. This type of supervision was indeed added as many former graduates can attest.

Other faculty members who were employed in the 1930's included Miss Mary Sander, a graduate of the UT School of Nursing who was employed around January 1, 1935, until January 1939, and Miss Ruth Neil Murry. Miss Murry graduated from UT in June 1936 and was employed as Teaching Supervisor in Nursing for the obstetrical wards. Miss Murry's appointment, beginning January 1, 1938, was at the rate of $85.00 per month. Miss Alice Mildred Dukes was employed March 20, 1939 as Instructor of Nursing Arts. Miss Ethel Fay Burton, who had been medical and surgical supervisor, also

Ruth Neil Murry

taught Nursing Arts beginning in 1939 and continued until March 1943. In addition to the Educational Director, Miss Cunningham, Ruth N. Murry, and Alice Dukes, other faculty listed in 1939 were: Ermine Sloan, Supervisor of Surgical Wards; Mrs. Elizabeth Bonner, Supervisor of Pediatric Wards; Ella Lietzke, Teaching Supervisor for Pediatric Wards; and Anne Decker Taylor, Teaching Supervisor for Medical Wards. Many of the individuals noted as faculty and paid by the University provided nursing service and did not engage in direct instruction of students.

In February 1940, Dr. Hyman noted in a letter to the University Registrar that the School of Nursing's Science-Nursing Program tended "to discourage a large proportion of those who might complete two years of college work but to whom attendance at our Liberal Arts College is impossible or difficult." Effective that year, students wanting to obtain the degree of Bachelor of Science in Nursing could complete

two years of prescribed college courses at any accredited college and the three-year nursing curriculum and earn the BSN. There was no difference in the nursing portion of the curriculum for the degree or non-degree students.

The 1940's brought concern about preparation for impending war and resulted in participation in the war effort for all nursing educational programs. Nationally, a Nursing Council on Defense was formed in 1940. A national inventory of registered nurses was conducted in 1941 showing that there were 289,286 registered nurses in the United States and that only 173,055 were actively practicing. The American Red Cross, which was the official agency recruiting for the Army Nurse Corps, noted that 4,000 additional nurses were being requested to care for new Army recruits (*The US Cadet Nurse Corps*, 1950). Several methods were explored to increase the nurse supply for both the military and civilian sectors with the decision made to augment the total enrollment of the existing schools.

Public Law 146 was passed by Congress on July 1, 1941. This Federal Security Agency Appropriation Act was passed in "recognition of the role of nursing in national defense and in anticipation of a shortage of nurses." (Thomas Parran, Surgeon Gen., letter of July 19, 1941). The funds were to be used to increase the number of students in basic programs of nursing, prepare inactive nurses, and for postgraduate courses in special fields. Grants were available for established schools of nursing and other institutions concerned with education of nurses. Federal guidelines stated that participating schools should be accredited by a state board of nurse examiners, connected to, or an integral part of, a hospital with a daily average of at least 100 patients, and have an adequate educational staff and facilities for carrying out the program. All applicants to the nursing program were required to have a diploma from an accredited high school. The curriculum was to be reviewed for all those units necessary to conform with the best present practices of basic nursing education. Requirements for participation also included a health service and education program and well balanced weekly schedules for the students.

The UT School of Nursing, under Dr. O.W. Hyman's signature, submitted a request for $19,700.00 of Federal aid on August 22, 1941. The application showed the intent to expand enrollment from 235 students to 300. Miss Frances Cunningham, Educational Director, and Mr. J.F. Ward, John Gaston Hospital Superintendent, along with Dr. Hyman, were listed as the committee submitting the application. A federal allotment of $4,100.00 was approved for UT in September for education of 10 additional students over the following 10-month period. University correspondence indicates that at least two new faculty were employed and paid with the federal funds. The funds from the Training for Nurses (national defense) Act were awarded for three years and extended through June 1943. The amounts actually received by the University were never as much as requested or approved due to a discrepancy in the way students were counted by the school and by the federal government.

Miss Eugenia K. Spalding, Federal Nursing Education Consultant, visited the School of Nursing April 13, 1942 in an attempt to resolve some of the enrollment discrepancies. While actual admissions to the program increased, withdrawals apparently canceled any gains.

Miss Ethel F. Burton, Faculty 1941

Miss Spalding's report gives the following description of the School: Based on the contract between the University and John Gaston Hospital, the University takes the responsibility of employing and paying instructors and admitting students. The hospital pays subsistence and illness costs giving the students an allowance of $10.00 per month. "Although this is called a University School of Nursing, it appears that the curriculum is not set up as such. If a student receives a degree (and very few have, not more than four in any one year) it is granted from its School of Liberal Arts at Knoxville… The physical and biological science courses at Memphis are taught at the university by regular instructors in the medical school with little or no modification for the nursing students…" These courses did not meet needs of the student and had a large number of failures, particularly in chemistry. Miss Spalding noted that the clinical courses were improving, but in general the curriculum needed revision. "If a degree program is desired, the director or dean of the school should administer the whole program. This should not be done by the dean of administration in the university (note – Dr. Hyman). The worst feature of this school is its plan of organization. The educational director (note – Frances Cunningham) who is employed by the university and who is under the dean of administration (Dr. O.W. Hyman), really carries out the functions of the dean or director of the school. There is another person in charge of the school (note – Ella George Hinton),

Hannah Pederson, Class of 1941

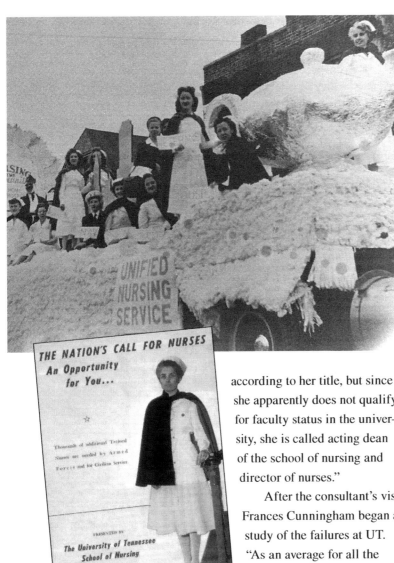

THE NATION'S CALL FOR NURSES
An Opportunity
for You...

Thousands of additional Trained
Nurses are needed by Armed
Forces and for Civilian Service.

PRESENTED BY

The University of Tennessee
School of Nursing
AND
The John Gaston Hospital
MEMPHIS, TENN.

*(top) World War II Nursing
float. R.N. Murry is pictured
far right
(above) Recruiting Brochure
(right) Cadet Nurse Recruiting
Poster*

and Frances Cunningham appointed Director of the School of Nursing. In actual practice, there appeared to be no change in the role and functions of the individuals.

Publicity in 1942 for the school noted the cost of the program to the student: "By their services to the hospital, pupil nurses earn their board, lodging, laundry, and ten dollars monthly. This is nearly enough to pay the cost of their education. About two hundred dollars additional is needed by the student during the three-year course — about half of this during the first six months."

Because of an anticipated shortage of nurses, it was decided that UT would operate the School of Nursing on a four-quarter plan effective Fall 1941. The expectation was to admit 30 students each quarter. Courses such as chemistry, microbiology, and materia medica had previously extended over more than a quarter but were changed so that the entire course was completed within one quarter. New faculty identified during 1941-1942 were: Mrs. Linda Darling, Evening Supervisor; Miss Esther McGlone, Social Sciences; Miss Mildred E.P. Miller, Nursing Arts; Miss Anne Messerly, Surgical Nursing; Mrs. Ruth D. Liddle, Medical Nursing; Miss Jane Smith, Dietetics; and Virginia Livesay, Surgical Nursing.

Miss Alice Dukes, Nursing Arts Instructor, resigned effective June 1941. Her letter stated that she felt her efforts were ineffective. "While I have closely adhered to methods of teaching and techniques approved by this school, they are not carried out in the ward situation, due primarily to the absence of necessary equipment, supplies, and personnel." Miss Cunningham, who was enrolled in

according to her title, but since she apparently does not qualify for faculty status in the university, she is called acting dean of the school of nursing and director of nurses."

After the consultant's visit, Frances Cunningham began a study of the failures at UT. "As an average for all the classes, I would say that we have been losing about 25% of our students. Failure is the cause of the large majority of these withdrawals." Reasons identified for the losses in 1941-42 were the change to a quarterly system and the readjustment of teaching schedules to correspond with that system and a new nursing arts instructor. The August 1942 application for funds listed administrative changes as: Ella G. Hinton, appointed Superintendent of Nursing Service,

FROM DIPLOMA TO DOCTORATE:

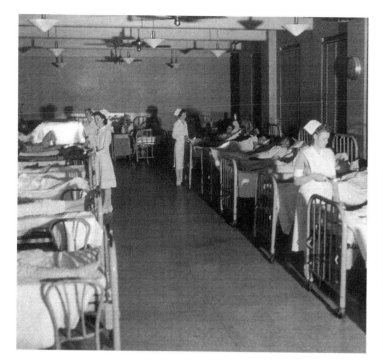

the master's program, attempted to recruit a replacement from Case Western Reserve. This applicant after her interview in Memphis wrote: "...It would be impossible for me to do the kind of teaching that I have in mind with your present equipment and setup." In a letter to Miss Cunningham, Dr. Hyman said, "if necessary lower your sights... I am afraid that we shall face several years of lower standards as the progress of war reduces availability of teachers." (May 13, 1941). Qualified faculty were employed, but the war did make the task of retention and recruitment more difficult. Many faculty changes occurred during this period with some individuals serving less than one year.

A number of UT graduates served in the military during the war. Of particular interest were two Army nurse graduates who were serving in the Philippines at the time of capture and were among those nurses known as "Angels of Bataan." Lieutenant Inez McDonald, a December 1934 graduate from near Tupelo, Mississippi, and Lt. Imogene Kennedy, a September 1940 graduate from

Philadelphia, Mississippi, were prisoners of war after the fall of Corregidor on May 6, 1942 until liberated in early 1945 (*The Commercial Appeal*, March 4, 1945).

On June 15, 1943, Public Law No. 74 was signed creating the uniformed US Cadet Nurse Corps. The nurse training legislation provided tuition, fees, uniforms, and monthly stipends to nursing students who agreed to make their services available for the duration of the war. The school also was paid for tuition and fees and maintenance during the first nine months of the educational program. All state accredited basic nursing schools were eligible to apply for the federal funds if they would accelerate the three-year program to 30 months and provide a period of full-time service for the senior Cadets in either a federal or non-federal hospital. The last six months before graduation, the Cadet provided full-time service to a hospital as if she were a graduate nurse (*US Cadet Nurse Corps*, 1950).

In August 1943, the University of Tennessee applied for a federal grant of $142,750.56 under the new Cadet Nurse Program. Dr. Hyman was

(left) John Gaston Hospital blackout, June 1942. Photo courtesy Mississippi Valley Collection, University of Memphis
(right) Students in front of Marcus Haase, January 1942

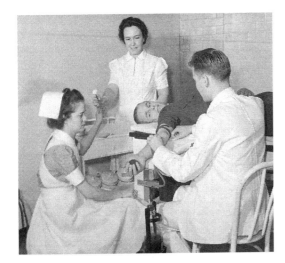

(top left) Margaret Patterson assists with blood transfusion. Photo from 1943 University of Tennessee Volunteer (above) UT Cadet Nurses Lorain Boshart, Helen Rigler, Mary Louise Pack, graduates of September 1944 (right) Dr. Morrison and students in chemistry laboratory

notified of tentative approval of those funds by telegram from Thomas Parron, Surgeon General (September 10, 1943). The first funding period extended to June 30, 1944. While exact numbers of UT students who participated are not available, it is apparent a large group chose to enroll in the Cadet Program.

The Cadet Program was not designed to reform nursing education in the US, but every effort was made to protect the use of federal funds and to avoid the lowering of standards. The application submitted by each school described educational, clinical and health resources. Regulations were given for participation that included such areas as adequate clinical experiences in medicine, surgery, pediatrics, and obstetrics and "well-balanced weekly schedules

of organized instruction, experience and study" (*US Cadet Nurse Corps,* 1950, p. 47). In an August 28, 1943, letter to Dr. Hyman, Eugenia Spalding, nursing education consultant for the U.S. Public Health Service Division of Nursing stated: "We note that the average weekly hours of practice and class for the junior and senior Cadet periods varies from 50 to 62 hours. These are excessive in comparison with the weekly average of 48 which is recommended." Total hours for UT students were reduced.

Another change brought about by the program had to do with marriages. Cadet Nurses were allowed to be married provided they continued their education until graduation and continued to serve as nurses until the end of the war. The John Gaston Hospital had not allowed

the marriage of any student nurse but changed their policy, "provided that they comply with rules and regulations of the hospital" (L.W. Dean, John Gaston Hospital to O.W. Hyman, UT, Nov. 12, 1943). Some of the Cadets served their last six months before graduation in a federal hospital such as Kennedy Army Hospital in Memphis. One student served at an Indian reservation hospital. The last class admitted to the Cadet program was in the Fall of 1945 (*US Cadet Nurse Corps*, 1950).

The end of World War II did not end the increased demand for nurses. Many military nurses did not return to their pre-war jobs in general hospital duty because of the increased responsibility they had in the WWII military and the satisfaction experienced in more

flexible, autonomous roles. WWII brought many changes in nursing. War resulted in hospitals employing people with little preparation, such as practical nurses and nurses' aides, to do routine and repetitive procedures. Nurses who served in the military were eligible for the GI Bill for education and many returned for advanced nursing preparation.

Post-war admissions to most US nursing schools declined. A UT School of Nursing report in 1949 noted there were 75 students enrolled in the school. Withdrawal rates were also high. Faculty and administrators believed the low number of admissions at UT was influenced by the type of patients cared for in John Gaston Hospital (low income, minority) as compared to schools affiliated with private

(top left) Post war student party at the University Center
(top right) 1948 graduates
(above) Traditional Capping ceremony, 1947

*Uniforms from 1920s-1948.
Modeled by class of 1949.*

hospitals. Because of this concern, the type of patient at John Gaston was discussed with all applicants at the time of their personal interview.

All students in 1949 had experience in medical, surgical, obstetric, pediatric, psychiatric, communicable disease nursing, and in the outpatient department. Annually, 12 students had a two-month experience in the city-county health department. Each student had five months each of medicine and surgical nursing supervised by the clinical instructor in each service. The operating room experience was six to eight weeks in length and diet kitchen was four weeks.

Other clinicals included: pediatrics, three months; obstetrics, 12 weeks; isolation, one month; and psychiatry, eight weeks. John Gaston Hospital was the primary clinical site and at that time consisted of 550 beds. The Gailor Psychiatric Hospital, which was completed in Spring 1948 and occupied the

top three floors and basement of the Thomas F. Gailor Hospital, was the clinical site for psychiatric nursing. Outpatient services were also housed in the Gailor.

In the late 1940's and early 1950's, UT was one of the better diploma programs in the country. An Interim Classification of Schools of Nursing in 1949 reported in the *AJN* in November of that year and the school data analysis in *Nursing Schools at the Mid-Century* (1950), rated UT in Group I, or the upper 25 percent, of basic programs in nursing in all areas except student health. The areas where UT failed to meet standards included excessive afternoon and night duty for the students, an average week of 48 hours of class, laboratory, and clinical instead of the recommended maximum of 44 hours (Murry to Hyman, Nov. 7, 1949).

The following is a comparison made by UT around 1950-51 to the "good school in 1949" from the *Nursing Schools at the Mid-Century:*

1950 Nursing School Curriculum Comparison

Good School of Nursing	UT School of Nursing
ORGANIZATION:	
Director appoints faculty: Independent budget prepared and administered by Director	Dean appoints faculty: Independent budget prepared and administered by Dean
FACULTY:	
Minimum of BS Degree. Not responsible for teaching more than 4 subjects. In school of 200 students, provide over 5000 hours teaching time per year for organized instruction	Minimum of BS Degree. Not responsible for teaching more than 4 subjects. In school of 120 students, provided over 1524 hours teaching time to 3 yr. students and 2636 hours of teaching time to 4 yr. students
HEALTH:	
44 hr. week. Not over 8 wks. night duty. Not over 8 wks. afternoon duty. Annual 4 weeks vacation. 3 wks. sick leave. PE before admission and annually; x-ray semi-annually.	48 hour week, except when on night duty and then night duty time plus class time. Vacation: total of 10 weeks for 3 yr. students and 16 weeks for 4 yr. students, 2 weeks sick leave allowed 3 yr. students and 3 for 4 yr. PE before admission and annually; x-ray semi-annually
CURRICULUM:	
250 hrs. physical and biological sciences with 120 hrs. of lab; 165 hrs. of social sciences; 1000 hrs. of med. sciences, nursing, allied arts, and clinical instruction	4 YR. STUDENT: 286 hrs. of physical and biological sciences with 286 hrs. of lab; 395 hrs. of social sciences; 1669 hrs. of med sciences, nursing, allied arts, and clinical instruction
	3 YR. STUDENT: 305 hrs. of physical and biological sciences with 49 hrs. of lab; 201 hrs. of social sciences, 969 hrs. of med sciences, nursing, allied arts, and clinical instruction

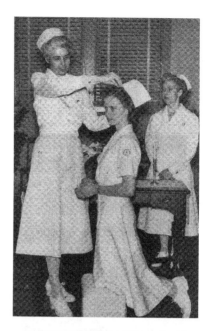

(top) Traditional Capping Ceremony (bottom) Three School Pins, Hospital Trustees medal, and Faculty medal

CHAPTER FOUR

The Baccalaureate Program and National Accreditation 1 9 5 0 - 1 9 7 1

A major administrative change in the nursing program came with the resignation of Miss Cunningham in February 1944. Miss Ruth Neil Murry was promoted from Assistant in Nursing to Assistant Professor and named Educational Director of the School of Nursing effective February 1, 1944. Her salary was advanced to $2,400 annually.

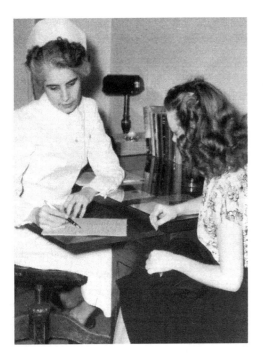

Miss Murry counseling with student

Miss Murry had served as a faculty member since 1938. She received her BS degree from the UT School of Nursing in 1940 based on her previous college work at Pearl River Jr. College and Mississippi Southern College in addition to the three year nursing program. In 1946 her title was changed from Educational Director to Director of the School of Nursing. By this time, there were eight full-time faculty in the school. Under Miss Murry's leadership, the School of Nursing became an autonomous unit within the University in July 1949, and she was appointed as its first Dean, with the rank of full professor. However, the home base for the school remained in the hospital, where students were provided a stipend and a residence (Murry, 1961).

A major study of nursing was conducted by Dr. Esther Lucile Brown in 1947-1948, which called attention to the need for collegiate preparation for nurses. At the 1949 National League for Nursing Education (NLNE) convention, the statement was made that there were at present approximately 90 basic nursing programs or

eight percent of all state accredited schools under university control. While the goal was to see more nursing programs as autonomous departments, it was recognized that "… just to link one's name with a university or college does not guarantee academic respectability or ensure a sound education basis for nursing students." (Goodale, 1949, p. 229). The School of Nursing at UT achieved the autonomous status in 1949, yet remained linked to the hospital.

In September 1950, the newly established Baccalaureate in Nursing Program admitted 26 students. The program was set up on a four-calendar-year basis, or 16 quarters, initially. Students continued to be admitted to the diploma or certificate program until the last group graduated in December 1954. In this early 1950's period, potential students applied for the four-year integrated program leading to a BSN, the three-year certificate program, or the degree program for those who had attended an accredited college for two years of approved courses. In this last option, the nursing curriculum was the same as that of the three-year certificate program. Students were admitted to the most appropriate of the three programs following the faculty admissions committee's review of the applicant's academic record, interview, and scores on the Henmon Nelson and California tests. The committee attempted to enroll anyone qualified into the newly developed baccalaureate program. Male students were admitted for the first time in the Fall of 1950 to any of the three options. Faculty minutes indicated the men lived in the old University dormitory with the medical students. Initially, male students had some lectures, demonstrations and practice in nursing arts and obstetrics apart from female students, and men had increased time in urology, orthopedics and psychiatry (faculty minutes, 1950). Mr. Charles William Yoakum was admitted to the three-year diploma program in 1950 and graduated in September 1953 as the first male graduate.

The difficult transition from a diploma to a baccalaureate program began as result of a statewide survey by the state nurses association demonstrating that the need for baccalaureate graduates in the state was not being met. At that time, the only baccalaureate nursing program in the state was offered by Vanderbilt University, a private school in Nashville. The UT nursing faculty reviewed the resources available on the Memphis campus to support the new program. With the exception of human anatomy and physiology, basic science instruction continued to be offered by faculty in those University departments. Clinical facilities continued to be available through the contract with the city hospital, John Gaston. Students paid fees to the University the first six quarters, but their maintenance still was provided by the hospital in return for services. Miss Murry (1961) reported that an obstacle for the baccalaureate program was the great distance between the liberal arts campus in Knoxville and the medical units campus in Memphis. Academic work in liberal arts was arranged through the University's extension program which isolated the nursing students from other college students.

In September 1949, Grace Spice (Wallace), a native of Canada, joined the UT faculty as assistant clinical instructor at Gailor Psychiatric Hospital. In September 1950, Mrs. Grace Wallace became an Assistant Professor. She taught Anatomy and Physiology to the nursing

students for many years, and in 1960 was appointed Assistant to the Dean coordinating admissions. Mrs. Wallace served in this capacity until her retirement in 1976.

In September 1951, 30 students were admitted to the baccalaureate program. Miss Emma B. Humphrey was employed as Director of Clinical Instruction. In this position, she worked closely with nursing service personnel in planning the clinical rotation of students, with the faculty in organizing and conducting their clinical teaching, and with the students to bring about improvements in the clinical teaching program. In this same year, Miss Lily Lusk acted as Director of the Nursing School for

(top) Grace Spice around 1949
(bottom) Brochure announcing Baccalaureate Degree Program

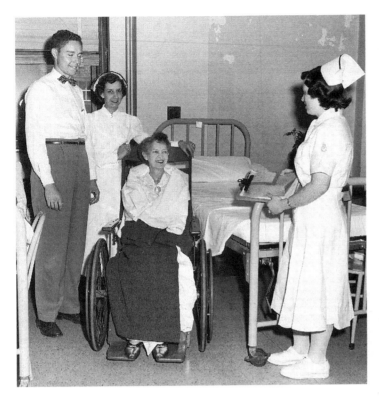

(left) 1950's John Gaston Hospital scene
(right) UT Nurses Basketball Team 1953-54

three-and-a-half months during Miss Murry's recovery from a major automobile accident.

Temporary accreditation was awarded to the baccalaureate program in 1952 by the National Nursing Accrediting Service. This accrediting service was formed in 1949 and discontinued in 1952 when accreditation became a function of the Division of Education of the newly formed National League for Nursing. The School of Nursing was not eligible for full accreditation until the baccalaureate program had been in effect for at least three years.

The 1952 accreditation was based on the completion of a questionnaire and a visit by a representative of the National Nursing Accrediting Service. The accreditation report was completed August 6, 1951, and identified the following strengths of the school: (1) UT facilities for science, (2) excellent clinical facilities on a contractual basis with John Gaston Hospital, and (3) autonomous unit in the state university. Plans identified in the report to augment or to improve the strength of the faculty included: (1) leave of absence for advanced study,

(2) improved faculty organization and conferences, and (3) better orientation programs.

The school also planned a more extensive counseling and guidance program, more lab experience in anatomy and physiology and microbiology, and more clinical conferences on specialties. A weakness brought out by the accreditation standards was the low percentage of nursing faculty with a master's degree. Of the nine full-time faculty identified, only two had a master's degree. Attrition of students in both the diploma and baccalaureate programs was another problem. By the time of the written report, two classes had been admitted to the BSN program, but apparently only 16 students remained.

In the early 1950's, the nursing students continued to devote a significant amount of time to patient care at the City Hospital. Faculty minutes of March 5, 1951, recorded that student nurses furnished two-thirds of the nursing care on hospital wards while graduate and practical nurses provided only one third. Even though the School of Nursing was limited by the 50-year contract with the city that controlled

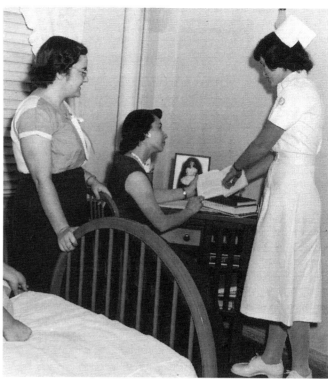

the administration of the nursing program, the faculty attempted to develop reasonable policies governing the hours of hospital work. These included: (1) students could not work more than 10 hours including class any day, (2) students could not be put in charge of a ward prior to their senior year, and (3) evening (after 7 p.m.) and night duty was not to exceed that recommended by the Mid-Century Report. (Faculty minutes, July 26, 1951).

Not every student hour was spent in study and work. Social activities in 1950 included student planned Halloween and Thanksgiving parties, a pajama party, softball games, and volleyball games. For the first time in 1950, a basketball team known as The University of Tennessee Nurses participated in the Memphis Nurses League. Previous teams had carried the name of the hospital. Games with Baptist, Methodist, and St. Joseph Schools of Nursing were played at the Gaston Community Center on Third Street. There was a student organization and a student paper called the "Gaston Gazette." Students also participated in the Memphis

Student Nurses Organization and "tea day" on Thursdays. Faculty noted in their meeting on November 1, 1950, the general opinion that the students should not have so many dances.

Up to 1953 the physical facilities used by the School of Nursing were housed in the hospital buildings and the Marcus Haase residence. Miss Murry's office was located on the first floor of John Gaston Hospital. Clinical instructors were based in the appropriate hospital site (Clinical Instructor in Pediatrics on the second floor of Tobey Children's Hospital, Clinical Instructor in Medicine on the third floor of John Gaston, Clinical Instructor in Surgery on the fourth floor of John Gaston, and Clinical Instructor in Obstetrics on the first floor of Maternity Hospital). Offices for the Nursing Arts Instructor and Assistant Instructor were located on the first floor of the Nurses' Residence as were the Nursing Arts practice room and laboratory. One classroom was available in the residence and one in the basement of John Gaston Hospital. Based on an inventory prepared by Miss Murry in July 1951, all of the nursing arts equipment,

(left) Student party scenes in the early 1950's
(right) A room in the Marcus Haase Residence

Classroom scene

classroom furnishings, and space as well as many of the office furnishings, were provided by the hospital. However, an expansion of the hospital administrative staff required the space devoted to the Dean and to some of the faculty of the nursing school. The Dean's office moved temporarily to a suite in the Marcus Haase Residence late in 1952. Forced to find space for the school, Dr. O.W. Hyman proposed the purchase of a house at 817 Court. The purchase of the old boarding house was authorized by the UT Board of Trustees on March 16, 1953. This building was considered temporary and was the first University building dedicated solely to the use of the School of Nursing. Dean Ruth Neil Murry, the secretarial staff and some faculty moved into the building. Open house was held November 19, 20, and 21, 1953. At the time of the move, the school had 15 full-time faculty and three part-time. Usually, two faculty shared an office in the eight-room house. Some faculty continued with offices on the hospital wards and in the Marcus Haase Residence because 817 Court was not large enough for the entire group.

The addition of the basic baccalaureate program was only one of the programmatic and curricular changes in the early 50's. The Post Graduate Course in Anesthesia again became operational with the admission of students in July 1951. Although listed as a nursing offering, this program was controlled by the Department of Anesthesiology. An annual report in 1952 noted 11 students had been admitted and five completed that year. However, problems were identified such as the limited number of applicants and poor performance of some of those who were accepted. The program was terminated at the end of Winter Quarter 1960 (NLN self-study question follow-up, 1960).

In September 1952, postgraduate courses in pediatric nursing and in psychiatric nursing were authorized by the campus and approved by the Board of Trustees on March 16, 1953. The four-quarter program that provided a Postgraduate Certificate in Nursing of Children was discontinued in the fall of 1954. Mrs. Mary Watkins, who came in 1952, taught the postgraduate psychiatric nursing courses. USPHS funds were

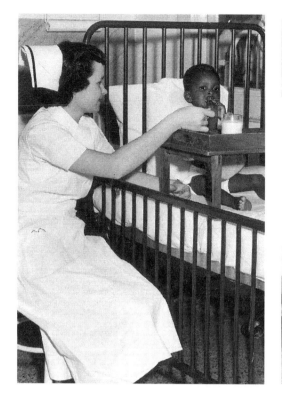

received to support a 12-month program in Psychiatric Nursing with baccalaureate level courses that could be applied toward the baccalaureate degree in nursing. The four-quarter postgraduate psychiatric nursing program ended September 30, 1958.

The Bachelor of Science in Nursing program for registered nurses (RN) also was approved on campus in September 1952. This was an eight-quarter program that included liberal arts and advanced nursing. The first RN students enrolled in the Winter Quarter 1953. For the most part, RN students attended classes with the basic students. RN students took additional nursing courses such as Curriculum, Principles of Teaching and Clinical Instruction. This baccalaureate program for registered nurses was intended to meet the need of Tennessee nurses to be better prepared for head nurse and teaching positions. The Barnes Report in 1949 had identified these as needs, and a survey in 1951 supported the same needs. (RN Murry to Hyman, Feb. 9, 1952).

New programs required additional faculty.

Miss May Sanders was employed as Director of the Postgraduate Nurse Program effective July 1, 1953, and Miss Dorothy Griscomb came on May 20, 1953, as a hospital based instructor. Miss Mildred Howard was employed as the school's first full-time Instructor in Public Health effective March 1, 1953.

Miss Dorothy Hocker came in January 1954, and Mrs. Mary Campbell became a clinical instructor in Pediatrics in September 1954. Mrs. Louise Rapp joined the faculty in 1955 to teach foundations of nursing. An April 1955 report listed 13 full-time nurse faculty and four part-time nurse instructors. Three of the part-time personnel were supervisors of nursing service within the hospital. By the end of 1955, only one instructor (operating room) was employed jointly by the school and hospital nursing service. Miss Murry noted that eight of the full-time faculty members had master's degrees; however, not all of those master's degrees were in nursing. The baccalaureate curriculum in 1955 was as follows:

Some of the liberal arts courses, such

(left) Pediatric Hospital scene (right) Miss Dorothy Hocker, second from right, and students from December 1956 class

First Year	1ST TERM		2ND TERM
English Composition	3	Physiological Chemistry	4
Inorganic/Organ Chemistry	4	English Composition	3
Biology	6	Biology	5
Intro. to Nursing	1	Intro. to Nursing	1
Intro. to Psychology	3	General Psychology	3

	3RD TERM		4TH TERM
Inorg/Organ Chemistry	5	Bacteriology	3
English Composition	3	Nutrition	3
Human Phys/Anatomy	7	Human Anat./Physics	7
Personality Development	3	Intro. to Public Health	2
		Intro. to Pharmacology	2
		Prin. of Nursing	3

Second Year	1ST TERM		2ND TERM
Pharmacology	4	Medicine & Surgery	6
Medical & Surg. Nursing	6	Principles of Nursing	4
Principles of Nursing	6	Sociology	3
Sociology	3		

	3RD TERM		4TH TERM
Social Case Work	3	English Literature	3
Public Speaking	3	Psychiatric Nursing	13
English Literature	3	Neurology	1
Medicine & Surg. Nursing	10		

Third Year	1ST TERM		2ND TERM
Medicine & Surgery	14	Obstetric Nursing	12
American Literature	3	American Government	3
		Princip. of Economics	3

	3RD TERM		4TH TERM
Elem. of Prev. Med/PH Statistics	3	Trends in Nursing	3
Pediatric Nursing	14	Role of PH Nurse	4
		Medicine & Surgery	9

Fourth Year	1ST TERM		2ND TERM
Comm. Hospital Exp.	3	Problem Solving	3
Medicine & Surgery	7	Medicine & Surgery	9
		History of West Civil.	3

	3RD TERM		4TH TERM
Ward Administration	3	Oppor. & Resp. in Nursing	2
History of US	3	Elective Practice	9
Medicine & Surgery	9	History of U.S.	3

as English, were conducted at the School of Nursing but taught by faculty employed for the specific subject. Chemistry, bacteriology, and pharmacology were taught by the UT School of Biological Science faculty. The Department of Psychology taught the psychology and person- ality development courses and participated in the psychiatric nursing courses. The Knoxville based School of Social Work taught the Social Case Work course. The UT Extension was used for public speaking, government, history, and economics courses. This pattern of instruction was followed from the beginning of the BSN program until 1958. Physicians provided classes for preventive medicine, pediatrics, psychiatry, neurology, orthopedics, gynecology, ENT, ophthalmology, obstetrics, urology, and general medicine and surgery.

A four-week community nursing clinical experience in Obion County, Tennessee, began in 1954 and continued until 1960 as a part of the baccalaureate curriculum. This experience included giving complete care to a small number of patients in Obion County General Hospital for four hours per day, six days each week (a total of 24 hours). Each afternoon students participated in community activities. Students lived in private homes and were expected to participate in professional, social, and religious activities. Observation visits were made in a physician's office, the county welfare department and civic clubs as well as visits with sanitarians (health department environmentalist), public health nurses, and home demonstration agents. Students also had a public health field experience in Memphis with the Visiting Nurses' Association for eight weeks.

In August 1955, Marie Buckley, a March 1937 graduate of UT School of Nursing, joined the faculty as Director of Clinical Instruction. She came from Vanderbilt where she had been Chairman and Associate Professor of Surgical Nursing. In addition to working with the clinical faculty, Miss Buckley taught several classes in clinical nursing, supervised clinical practice, and taught a course in professional nursing.

In 1955 a program for African-American nurses, called the City of Memphis Hospitals School of Nursing, was established at the E.H.

Marie Buckley

Crump Hospital and was administered by the City of Memphis. The first class of students was admitted in January 1956. From 1956 through 1958, UT assumed responsibility for classroom instruction in the diploma program until that school was able to secure qualified faculty. In addition to Crump Hospital, UT also provided instruction in psychiatric nursing for other diploma schools including Baptist Hospital School of Nursing.

A significant event occurred when application was made for full accreditation from the National League for Nursing (NLN). League consultants visited the school February 18-23, 1957, and the school's written report was submitted to NLN in the same year. The program was denied accreditation at the April 1957 meeting of the Collegiate Board of Review. Reasons given for the denial included:

1. A large number of faculty without master's degrees.

2. The contract between the University and the City of Memphis Hospitals related to clinical experience for students was not considered educationally sound.

3. Clinical experience in some areas was not considered educational.

4. Courses in general education needed to be given in a College where students would have an opportunity to meet with students and instructors in disciplines other than nursing.

Margaret Bridgeman, NLN consultant from the Department of Baccalaureate and Higher Degree Program, described the situation of the school in her report of November 1957:

Although it has been called the University of Tennessee School of Nursing for thirty-one years, it has been able to devote entire attention to senior-college

Marcus Haase Dorm

level education for the profession for only the last three. It is far from surprising that full national accreditation for the program was not achieved in so short a time, although so much progress had been made that the School was approved for a survey. The faculty should not be discouraged because arrival at this hoped-for goal has been deferred. The advancement of any type of education to a higher level always involves difficulties and, in nursing, the transition from hospital school policies to those characteristic of university education presents special problems. Furthermore, the particular situation of the University of Tennessee School of Nursing imposes conditions which make the process harder. In such a situation, it is apparent that a school needs the utmost assistance and support from the university which is responsible for it and of which it is an integral part.

Golden Williams, who was Secretary-Consultant from the Tennessee Board of Nursing, met with Dean Ruth Neil Murry regarding accreditation on February 6, 1958.

A recommendation from that meeting stated: "The present contract requiring students to provide service for patients in the City of Memphis Hospitals is contrary to accepted educational policies for degree programs in nursing. It is strongly recommended that this contract be changed to allow faculty members to control student experience in the clinical areas, and the amount of time students spend in the clinical areas should be determined by student needs." As a result of the NLN and State Board recommendations, the 50-year contract between the University and the City of Memphis Hospitals over administration of the School of Nursing was amended. Students were required to pay for their own maintenance and were released from nursing service responsibilities. For the first time, the School of Nursing became truly autonomous.

Contract negations between the hospital and The University of Tennessee gave the School of Nursing faculty full responsibility for planning and control of student learning experiences. The clinical practice of students was first reduced to 24 hours a week and then to approximately 20 hours per week as of January 1, 1960. Initially, the school agreed to an obligatory paid service of eight hours per week by each student in the tenth and succeeding quarters. This agreement was altered in January 1960 so that employment of students by nursing service was voluntary.

Housing for nursing students improved in 1958 when the Marcus Haase Nurses' Home was totally remodeled, and a new entrance added on Jefferson, changing the address from 860 Madison (rear) to 885 Jefferson. A formal opening was held on November 22, 1958. Housing and meals had been provided by the hospital until the contract with the city was altered requiring students to provide their own maintenance beginning January 1958. Students paid rent to the hospital. Nursing students lived in the Marcus Haase residence until the University opened the new Randolph

dormitory for all students on campus in July 1969.

A major curriculum change occurred in 1958 in an attempt to correct a problem cited in the accreditation visit. Students were admitted only after completion of one year of prescribed course work from an accredited college. Previously, the students had been admitted directly to the UT campus, and instruction was purchased for them. As pointed out in the accreditation report and the consultation visit, this did not allow the nursing students an opportunity for campus life with other undergraduate students. In 1958-59 students were enrolled jointly at Memphis State University and UT. They lived on the Memphis State campus, and one of the UT Nursing faculty went there to teach a three-quarter-hour course in Foundations in Nursing. The joint enrollment was discontinued when a large number of freshman students applied with no nursing courses for the 1959-60 school year. These students transferring from other colleges were taught a three week concentrated course in the summer prior to the

sophomore year. This freshman year nursing content was incorporated into the second year courses in 1960. After enrollment in the School of Nursing, the students continued taking liberal arts courses on the campus of Memphis State their sophomore and junior years. One problem experienced by the nursing faculty and students in this new arrangement was the difference in term organization — a quarter system at UT and a semester system at Memphis State. Furthermore, vacation or term break periods were never the same! The length of the total program was reduced to 15 quarters in 1957, and to 14 quarters (including the one academic year of prerequisites) for the class graduating June 1962. In the fall of 1960, there were 80 students enrolled in the generic program and eight in the general program for RN's.

Alteration of the curriculum for registered nurses leading to a BSN occurred in 1958. Specialization was discontinued with the program essentially the same learning experiences for the RN's and generic students. Effective September 1959, a transition quarter of study was provided for the RN's in the fall, followed

Students learning anatomy with the famous "Bone Box," 1959

Dr. Mary Morris

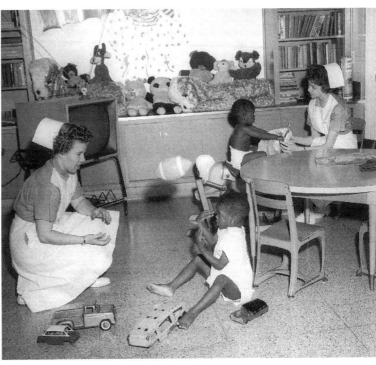

(left) Dorothy Hocker and
Ruth Neil Murry
(right) Tobey Hospital Scene
with Sarah Hall (Gueldner)
'62 and Marjorie
McCullum '63

*Grace Wallace,
Assistant to the Dean*

by two quarters with the generic students. All RN's completed prescribed courses in liberal arts and at least the senior year on the UT campus. The National League for Nursing Graduate Nurse Qualifying Examination was required for all of the RN's. If deficiencies were identified based on the test, additional courses were required in deficient areas.

Bridgeman (1957) noted in her report that the need for nursing college faculty members had suddenly and greatly increased in the last 10 years. Even though nationally there was a shortage of qualified faculty, Dean Murry recruited additional faculty with master's degrees and provided opportunities for current faculty to take leaves for advanced study. Mrs. Mildred Proctor, a graduate of 1928, joined the faculty in 1957 to teach public health nursing; Mrs. Katherine Lutes joined in 1958 to teach psychiatric nursing; and Miss Mary Morris came in 1959 to teach medical-surgical nursing. A total of 16 full-time faculty members were listed in the 1959 accreditation report. The February 1960 NLN visitors' report noted that eight of these faculty members had a master's

degree with nursing preparation and four had master's degrees in other fields. The remaining four faculty had the baccalaureate as their highest degree. The administrative organization of the faculty was restructured in 1960 to consist of six heads of departments. Miss Dorothy Hocker became head of Medical and Surgical Nursing; Mrs. Mary Campbell became head of Nursing of Children; Miss Constance Lemerand became head of Maternity Nursing; Mrs. Katherine Lutes became head of Psychiatric Nursing; Miss Mildred Howard became head of Public Health Nursing; and Miss Marie Buckley became head of General Nursing (RN completion program). Miss Murry continued as Dean, and Mrs. Grace Spice Wallace became her Assistant.

The School of Nursing applied again for NLN accreditation in 1959 and was visited on February 14-20, 1960. In a letter dated May 31, 1960, from the NLN Collegiate Board of Review, Dean Murry was notified of the granting of accreditation to the baccalaureate basic program and the general nursing program for RN's, both with public health nursing. A progress report was to be submitted for the

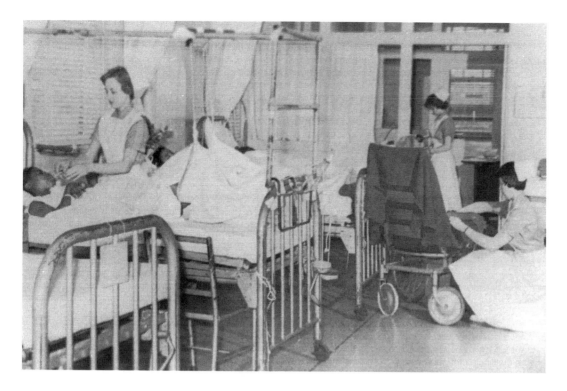

John Gaston Hospital scene 1961-62

Spring 1963 meeting of the Board. Recommendations from the accreditation included:

1. The College of Nursing employ sufficient full-time nurse faculty who are prepared through graduate preparation in the special curriculum area in which they teach in numbers that will guarantee a suitable ratio of faculty to student.

2. The faculty continue to explore additional facilities in order to provide learning experiences with patients from varied socioeconomic backgrounds.

3. The faculty continue to explore additional facilities in order to provide learning experiences… with maternity patients where they may observe the development of mother-child relationship and opportunity for parent education beyond the immediate post-partum period. (Editor's Note: City Hospital policies for care of newborn infants limited nursing students' opportunities for learning about mother-child relationship and patient teaching. Immediately after birth, infants were admitted to the nursery and did not come out to the mother for any visitations or feedings.)

4. The faculty in the departments of maternity nursing, nursing of children, and public health nursing coordinate their efforts to develop a dynamic experience in 521N that would enrich this course.

The principle clinical resources used by the school in 1960 included: the City of Memphis Hospital units of John Gaston Hospital for medical and surgical nursing and obstetrics; Tobey Memorial Hospital for pediatrics and Out-Patient Department; the Memphis and Shelby County Health Department for public health nursing; and Thomas F. Gailor Memorial Hospital for psychiatric nursing. All facilities were located within a two-block area of the nursing school. A typical week of a nursing student in clinical nursing courses was described in the following manner: "The ninth quarter student's week includes three hours of academic work and seven hours of nursing theory concurrent with twenty hours of laboratory practice. Practice includes conferences and field trips.

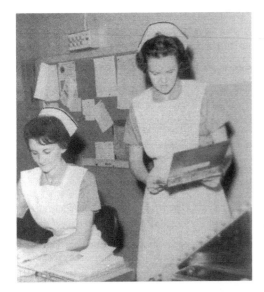

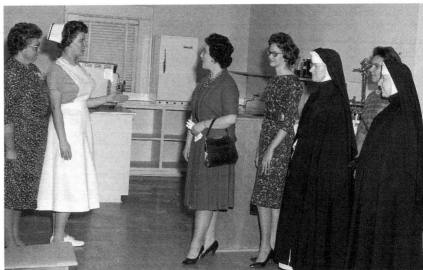

879

(top left) John Gaston Hospital scene 1961-62
(top right) Dr. Mary Morris and Mary Ann Barbee '62 showing new nursing arts lab at Lindsley Hall open house 1962
(bottom left) Marilyn Dunavant '66 at entrance to Lindsley Hall
(bottom right) Lindsley Hall – formerly College of Physicians & Surgeons Building – College of Nursing Building 1962-1973

Two hours of preparation for each class gives the student a fifty hour weekly schedule." (*Report of UT School of Nursing* to NLN, June 1959, p.37)

In February 1961, the UT Board of Trustees voted to change the title of the program from School of Nursing to College of Nursing, and nursing was recognized as one of six colleges on the Medical Units campus. UT College of Nursing was one of the four basic baccalaureate programs in the state. The other three were Vanderbilt School of Nursing in Nashville, Meharry Medical College School of Nursing in Nashville, and East Tennessee State College

in Johnson City. The UT College of Nursing provided instruction in psychiatric nursing in Memphis for East Tennessee students according to contract. UT provided one full-time instructor for these students with money for salary coming from a grant through the Department of Psychiatry.

After many years of having offices of the Court Street house, the College moved into Lindsley Hall at 879 Madison on August 25, 1961. Lindsley Hall, built in 1905, had been the old College of Physicians and Surgeons and then the headquarters of the Memphis and Shelby County Health Department. The inside of the building had been totally remodeled at a cost of $175,000. The newly remodeled building provided offices for all faculty and administrators, classrooms, a nursing laboratory, conference rooms, and a 116 seat auditorium. A dedication of the building was held on February 9, 1962, with Mrs. Judith L. Whitaker, Executive Secretary of the American Nurses' Association, serving as speaker. Faculty and students took great pride in the new College of Nursing building.

The February 1963 progress report to the NLN noted the following improvements to the College: three additional faculty members with master's preparation in nursing, and one with a PhD had been employed. Miss Morris and Miss Buckley had received post-master's diplomas from Teachers College, Columbia University. Miss Morris was also currently on leave to complete her EdD. In order to provide learning opportunities with patients from diverse socioeconomic backgrounds, clinical rotations included experiences at Le Bonheur Children's Hospital, Kennedy Veteran's Administration Hospital for care of patients with tuberculosis and chronic disease, and B'nai B'rith Home and Hospital for the Aged.

Opportunities for students to observe the development of the mother-child experience and to teach parents beyond the immediate post-partum period were provided by having students select a patient in the prenatal clinic. Students then followed the patient to make prenatal home visits; give care during the labor, delivery and post-partum period; and to make at least one post-partum visit. Also in public health nursing, students were assigned to families with at least one prenatal patient who would deliver during the quarter. Nursing 431 Seminar was a new course that included a team nursing experience, a general hospital receiving ward experience, and a nursing home experience. The Gailor Psychiatric Hospital discontinued inpatient services in May 1962.

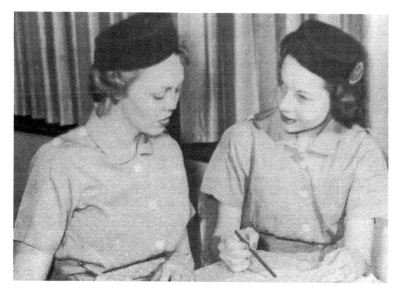

Clinical experiences for psychiatric nursing were changed to the new state-supported Tennessee Psychiatric Hospital and Institute.

Beginning in the late 1950's and in the decade of the 60's, the College of Nursing participated in several projects funded through the US Public Health Service. A psychiatric nursing grant for the purpose of coordinating psychiatric teaching in the total basic curriculum was initiated July 1957 and continued through August 1962. Miss Mary Watkins became the coordinator and a PhD clinical psychologist, Dr. Carl B. Smith, Jr., was employed to assist in evaluation and strengthening the

(top) Students preparing for home visits
(bottom) Public Health nursing class – Mildred Proctor and Rachel Taylor, faculty

(top) Pediatric scene-Florence Bright, faculty member (bottom) Dr. Ted May, Marjorie Keller, Dr. Mary Morris, and Miss Murry discuss Occupational Health Grant

Margaret Haynes was employed as project nurse of a "Training Program in Mental Retardation for Undergraduate Students in the UT College of Nursing." This project continued through 1971 and had as its purpose to evaluate and enrich the nursing curriculum to the content area of mental retardation and related handicapping conditions. A teaching-learning planning project funded by the Department of Health, Education & Welfare was initiated in 1971. This resulted in a three-year curriculum implementation grant for the purpose of individualizing student learning.

By the time of the 1968 National League for Nursing accreditation visit, there were 155 students and 24 full-time faculty. The College was seeking to increase the number of faculty who held a doctorate or were working on one. Research and writing also were given increased emphasis. The report proudly noted "nine articles by faculty had been published in nursing and non-nursing journals since 1965" (1968 *Self Evaluation Report*). Dr. Mary Morris received her EdD in Nursing from Teachers College in 1964 and became one of the first faculty members with a doctoral preparation in nursing. She provided leadership for a curriculum revision that was implemented in 1965. The revised curriculum focused on basic human needs and was organized into three years. In 1968 the College was accredited by the NLN with no recommendations.

Minority students were not a part of the UT Memphis College of Nursing until the 1960's. The first African-American graduate of the College was Grace McLeod, a registered nurse student from Nashville who graduated in June 1966. Two generic undergraduate African American students were admitted in the Fall of 1967 and graduated in June 1970. By the 1976 accreditation self-study report, there were 17 male students and 23 African American female students enrolled out of the total 273 students.

psychiatric content. Additionally, UT was selected as one of two sites in the US to conduct a curriculum project related to occupational health nursing. The project was initiated in February 1965 and continued for four-and-one-half years. Julia D. Smith, who joined the faculty as Chair of Public Health Nursing in September 1962, was project director, and Marjorie Keller was employed as principal investigator. The goals of the project were to identify occupational health content that was essential to baccalaureate nursing education and to develop methodology for evaluating such content in a curriculum (Keller, 1970). In 1967

WHY PROFESSIONAL NURSING ?

BECAUSE modern nursing is an exciting experience.

BECAUSE it offers an opportunity for personal involvement in a helping situation with individuals, families, and groups.

BECAUSE, as a contributing member of the health team, the professional nurse works with others and helps to meet the health needs of the rich and poor; sick and well.

BECAUSE the professional nurse has numerous occupational opportunities – providing, supervising and teaching nursing.

BECAUSE the professional nurse can continue academic study and prepare as a clinical specialist who commands depth knowledge in psychiatric, maternity, pediatric, medical and surgical, or public health nursing. The specialist is prepared to do research and function as a true leader in nursing.

WHY BACCALAUREATE NURSING ?

BECAUSE a college education with a nursing major offers social, cultural and educational advantages.

BECAUSE the social experience of college life is an educational process by itself.

BECAUSE the responsibility of the curriculum belongs to a university faculty, both nurse and non-nurse.

BECAUSE the background of humanities, social and physical sciences provide a foundation for depth nursing courses.

BECAUSE the graduate earns a college d...

WHY UNIVERSITY OF TENNESSEE COLLEGE OF NURSING ?

BECAUSE as a part of the Medical Units, the College of Nursing offers an opportunity to see the big picture and to participate with others in providing needed care through joint student learning experiences.

BECAUSE the college is a part of the Memphis Medical Center and located nearby downtown Memphis.

BECAUSE students have a wide variety of clinical nursing experiences at public, private, and community health agencies.

BECAUSE the well-qualified faculty is committed to helping the student grow personally and professionally.

BECAUSE the student is provided with learning experiences which form a foundation of nursing care based ...ples rather than rote prac...

...SE the learning experi... the student grow beyond ...l, psychological, and cul...ground and enable the ... function as a profession...

(top) Recruitment brochure
(center) Home visit
(right) Grace McLeod – first African-American graduate '66 (second from left) with M. Ousley, P. Toler, and medical intern

CHAPTER FIVE

Evolution of the College of Nursing Alumni Perspectives 1928-1970

The Early Years 1920s-1930s

BY MILDRED BIRKHEAD PROCTOR,* CLASS OF 1928

At a very early age, I had the experience of riding with my father in a horse and buggy as he visited patients in their homes in rural Arkansas. His concern and care of the ill must have made an impression on me, and influenced my decision to enter nursing. An epidemic of smallpox hit the community when I was two years old. My father, a 13-year-old sister, and I were the only survivors of a family of eight. My father died when I was eleven years old.

I graduated from high school and taught in a country school for two years before I decided to explore the possibility of being a nurse. I married a young country doctor who I helped in the office and accompanied on house calls. After my husband's untimely death, I talked with our family physician about studying nursing. He thought nursing would be a good choice for me and advised me to go the Memphis General Hospital. He said I would find it to be the best nursing school in the area. I made application to the school and was accepted. I have never been sorry I followed his advice.

On January 1, 1924, I found my way to the Memphis General Hospital, located on Madison Avenue where the John Gaston Hospital was built later. I found the Nursing Director's office and received a very warm welcome. After several questions and answers, I was escorted to the Nurse's Home

Mildred Proctor
faculty member

and introduced to the Matron for orientation to the living quarters. She showed me the room I was to occupy with another new student and showed me the other facilities in the home, including the commode. She demonstrated how to flush it. The home was a large three-story, white, wooden building located between the west end of the hospital and a fire station that faced Dunlap. Students were housed on the first and second floors. The third floor was a recreation area. The nurses' home was replaced by Marcus Haase Nurse's Residence while I was a student. While the new residence was being built, several students were housed in rooms located over a restaurant that faced Dunlap next to the fire station.

The Matron of the home stressed the importance of obeying the house rules and regulations. We were to be in our rooms at 9:00 p.m. — lights out at 10:00 p.m. — up and

(left) Memphis General Hospital School of Nursing Basketball team, Fall 1924. Mildred is holding the basketball
(below) Mildred Proctor as young student

dressed with beds made and room in order for inspection at 6:30 a.m. — and to breakfast and to report to our assigned ward at 7:00 a.m.

My next stop was the sewing room, located in the basement of the Hospital, where I was fitted for my probation uniform which consisted of a blue shirtwaist dress and white apron to be worn with black shoes and hose.

I joined a group of new students, and we were introduced to the only nursing instructor in the school. She demonstrated the use of the contents of a large wooden box (approximately 20 x 12 x 8 inches). It contained soap, rubbing alcohol, talcum powder, and wash cloths. We were told how we were to use the contents in giving a.m. and p.m. care to patients. We were to pick up the box each a.m. and p.m. and on returning it to replace the contents for use the next time.

The instructor then led us on a tour of the hospital pointing out the various departments such as x-ray, labs, supply room, pharmacy, and emergency rooms. On entering each ward, one or more of the students were introduced to the nurse in charge, and instructed to report to the ward each day at 7:00 a.m. The nurse in charge, who may have been a senior student, would be responsible for our daily assignment on the ward. In addition to a.m. and p.m. care, we learned we might be assigned to clean and sterilize bedpans, clean beds and bed-side tables, clean the hopper room, and count linens. We frequently were assigned these tasks.

A schedule was posted on each ward along with information on when to report to the instructor for further demonstrations and practice in the techniques and skills we needed to care for patients and for carrying out the orders of the doctors. We learned how to make beds — with and without patients — to take TPR's — to give bed baths — to give enemas — to catheterize patients — to make and apply

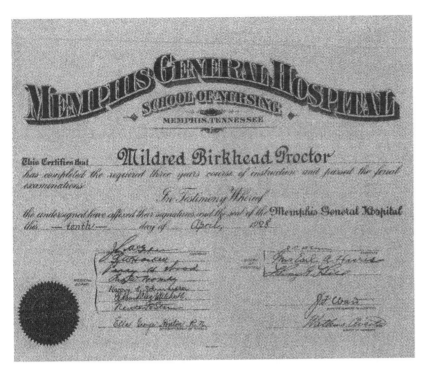

mustard plasters and turpentine stupes, which were used on patients with pleurisy or pneumonia. Little by little we learned to measure and give medications and do the charting. Our classes were all taught by doctors, except nutrition, which was taught by the author of the text we used.

We cared for patients with many diseases that are rarely seen today, since many discoveries in diagnosis and treatment of disease have reduced their incidence today. All childhood communicable diseases were seen frequently, as well as tuberculosis, typhoid fever, syphilis and other venereal diseases. An Isolation Hospital facing Jefferson Avenue was built during my second and third year in school.

Apparently there were very few students in the school who had any financial aid from home. We received $15.00 per month plus room, board and laundry for three years from the hospital. We had to pay for our own books, uniforms and personal items. It is difficult to believe that we managed to get by on that small amount, but we did.

New students were admitted every three months. Only single, white females were accepted. High school graduation was not required. There were a few that dropped out during the first few months. At the end of three months when new students arrived, we immediately were given more responsibility. Each of us was assigned to a ward for eight-hour daily duty. Classes were on our "off" hours. We often had split hours to accommodate the hours needed for classes. If we were on the 11:00 p.m. to 7:00 a.m. shift, we had to stay up, or get up, for class. As well as I can remember, there were few complaints about restrictions on our time.

My first assignment for eight-hour ward duty was to a female medical ward for the 3:00 p.m. to 11:00 p.m. shift. I remember feeling rather frightened to learn I would be the only nurse on the ward with over 20 patients. I had many questions for the evening supervisor when she made rounds. She checked the medications I had prepared and returned later to see if I needed more help.

At the end of six months, we were notified that our probation time was over. Our uniforms were changed to a blue and white-striped dress with white apron, bib, collar, cuffs, and cap. We continued to wear black shoes and hose for 3 years. The class ahead of us sponsored a "Capping Party" for us. It was held on the lawn outside the Pediatric Ward with children's chairs and tables. We enjoyed refreshments, played games, and much fun was had by all.

As we advanced and gained further knowledge of diseases and treatments, we were given more responsibility in management of the ward and the care of patients. Students were rotated through the wards and services and spent a certain amount of time in special areas such as the operating room, delivery room and pediatrics ward. The only OPD experience I recall was an assignment to assist in the syphilis clinic held each Saturday morning in Eve Hall which was located south of Madison Avenue behind Lindsley Hall.

In the operating room, maternity and pediatric wards, the head nurse was a registered nurse. The head nurse on some of the other wards was a senior student nearing graduation. This was a good experience and useful for me when I was adjusting to a position as an RN. The only help on the wards other than students was a maid and an orderly. We became acquainted with students from the other hospital schools by way of our basketball games. There was a lot of competition with students from Baptist, Methodist, and St. Joseph Hospital Schools as well as between the first-year students and the seniors in our own school.

The State Board of Nursing Examinations for registered nurse licensure were held in Rogers Hall, the UT College of Dentistry Building on Union Ave, west of Manassas Street. We spent two days taking 13 examinations. My first position as a registered nurse was as Head Nurse on a ward for white, male patients. My first salary was $100.00 per month plus room, board, and laundry. I thought I was rich!

I've worked in many areas of nursing, but have never lost my interest in trying to improve the health practice of those in need. The skills and techniques learned in my early years have been most useful throughout my 61 years in nursing. I have been asked many questions in the past few years. "What was nursing like when you first started?" "Why did you enter Nursing?" "How was your schooling paid for?" "What salary did you get in your first job as a registered nurse?" — Perhaps I have answered some of them.

*Mildred Proctor
1993*

*Mildred Birkhead Proctor *wrote the above description in 1991 at the request of Dianne Greenhill to provide a historical view of an early student's experience. Mildred was born January 4, 1902, in Butlerville, Arkansas. She received a diploma of nursing from the UT School of Nursing in 1928. After graduation Mildred worked as a Head Nurse at the Memphis General Hospital. She also worked as a staff nurse with the Metropolitan Life Insurance Company and for 11 years as the Supervisor of the Variety Club Mother's Milk Bank in Memphis. ✦ She served as a Navy nurse in World War II stationed at Portsmouth, Virginia. Her baccalaureate was awarded from Vanderbilt University in 1953 and her MA from Teachers College, Columbia University in New York in 1954. ✦ After graduate preparation, she was a public health nursing supervisor with the Baltimore, Maryland County Health Department. She joined the faculty of the UT School of Nursing in January 1957 as an Instructor of Public Health Nursing. ✦ Mildred was promoted to Assistant Professor and continued to teach in public health until her retirement from UT on August 31, 1970. Mildred supervised many students in their undergraduate clinicals at the Memphis & Shelby Co. Health Department. Mildred was active in the Tennessee Nurses Association, the American Public Health Association, and the Tennessee League for Nursing (TLN). She held the office of Treasurer in the TLN for many years. ✦ After her retirement, Mildred continued in public health, working in the local health department family planning clinic. She remained active in alumni activities and received the Most Supportive Alumnus Award in 1988. She later moved Jackson, Mississippi to be near her family. Mildred was living in Jackson when she died in May 23, 1995. At her request, she was buried in Memphis near her two sisters. ✦*

The Early Years 1920s-1930s

BY MARIE BUCKLEY,* CLASS OF MARCH 1937

I was born on Friday, August 13, 1915 in Carlisle, Arkansas and attended high school there, graduating in May 1933. In 1933 we were in the depths of a depression and there were no scholarships to go to college, so I knew I could not go to college and prepare to become a teacher. I was job hunting for weeks in Little Rock, but there were no jobs available. Our family dentist's daughter was a graduate of the University of Tennessee School of Nursing. She was a supervisor in the operating room at Memphis General Hospital. I talked with her many times, and she was so enthusiastic about her career. She brought materials home for me to study and an application for admission. It did not take long for me to choose UTSN over the three diploma schools of nursing in Little Rock on the basis of Ethelyn Arp's recommendation and the fact it was a University program. Little did I realize it was not a baccalaureate degree program in nursing.

When we were admitted to UTSN we were placed with other new students in the wings of the Marcus Haase Nurses' Home. There were about eight single beds placed side by side. By the end of the first six months (probationary period) there were about 24 of the 35 students left. A few had left within the first few weeks. We were gradually moved to double rooms. We had the traditional curriculum of the 30's. At UT the first nine months included instruction in Anatomy and Physiology taught by Dr. Cleveland S. Simpkins, Chairman of the Department; Chemistry taught by Dr. Dempsey Morrison, Chairman of the Department; Bacteriology taught by Dr. Max Lindsey; Pathology taught by Dr. I. D. Michelson, Chairman of the Department; Nutrition and Diet Therapy taught by noted author Dr. Fairfax Proudfet; Massage taught by Dr. E.D. Bohannon; Nursing Arts taught by Terry Brady; Materia Medica taught by Dr. Ettledorf; and Bandaging. It seemed to me that we were in class or labs five to six hours and four hours of clinical everyday. The biggest challenge was to dissect cadavers under Dr. Simpkins and then to feel like you smelled for formaldehyde the rest of the day.

Every morning at 6:15 we had to be in the Recreation Room for roll call, a prayer and general inspection of our uniforms and appearance. Our clinical activities included giving a.m. and p.m. care 7-9 a.m. and 5-7 p.m., and on Saturdays 7-11 a.m., we gave a.m. care

Marie Buckley

Marie Buckley, Assistant Dean, at Golden Apple Banquet; Dean Marie Joshberger in background

and then were responsible for cleaning all bedpans, urinals, and bedside units.

Our supervision for the School of Nursing was from Miss Laura Odell who walked in the center of the aisle and looked to the right and left never saying a word to students or patients. The head nurses and upperclassmen helped to answer all of our questions and showed us how to perform all of the procedures. Mostly, we learned by trial and error.

During the next two-and-one-half years, we received a monthly stipend of $10-$15 a month. We had classes in Medicine taught by Dr. James B. McElroy, Chairman; Surgery, Obstetrics and Gynecology taught by Dr. W.T. Pride, Chairman; Pediatrics, Orthopedics, EENT, Communicable Diseases and Public Health. All of our clinical classes were taught by physicians with the exception of Public Health. It is amazing to me that almost all of our classes were taught by the chairmen of departments. Public Health was taught by several nurses from the Health Department during the last quarter of school. They were Mrs. B.L. Cawthon, Mrs. Ruth

Huntly, and Miss Alice Frisz.

During the first year of our program, we went to physical education class 7-9 on Friday evenings. It was conducted by someone from the Memphis Park Commission. We wore white middies, black bloomers and stockings. We did some types of exercises and played basketball.

During the last two years of our program, we had three to six hours of classes a week and approximately 48 hours of clinical practice with a lot of overtime. There were no licensed practical nurses, nurses' aides or staff nurses. Each ward had a head nurse who worked eight hours a day for six-and-a-half days a week for a total of 52 hours. Student nurses staffed the entire hospital 24 hours a day, seven days a week. All of our clinical experiences were in Memphis General Hospital.

We spent hours and hours on repetitive tasks, such as cleaning beds, beside tables, washing and sterilizing equipment, folding linen from the laundry, squeezing oranges in the diet kitchen, folding surgical sponges, etc. I had about four months practice in the operating

(top) Mooney Library
(left) Isolation Hospital
(right) Great Hall of Mooney Library

room and three months in the Emergency Room because they needed me. By the time our class graduated, there were only seven out of the 35 students left. We all felt like the City and UT had used us as slaves. We were bonded to all UT graduates as our upperclassmen had been so kind, thoughtful and helpful to us in every way. We also felt proud that we had seen and done just about everything in the field of medicine.

There was little social life as we were so busy in the classrooms and the hospital that we had little time left to study. We had to be in every night at 8:30, except for Saturday and Sunday when we could stay out until 10:00 p.m. Mrs. Julia Funk, the matron, was a very stern German, and she made bed checks every night at 10. We could stay out until 11:00 p.m. one

Saturday evening a month to go to the University Center to attend an all-student dance. We had to sign in and out every time we left the dorm in the evening.

As we became juniors and seniors, we had more time to shop, go to movies, swim and date. We did not have to study for our three to six hours of classes except for midterm and final examination.

A very distinguished nurse educator, Frances Cunningham, became our Director of Education during my senior year. She had the knowledge, experience and interpersonal skills to make major changes in our curriculum and clinical practice. She employed two more faculty members, Ann Taylor and Ethel Fay Burton, to supervise clinical practice.

I graduated from UT in March 1937. Frances Cunningham had just started a new arrangement with the Memphis Shelby County Health Department whereby one or two students would have a three-month experience at the Department after graduation. I was the only student to apply for this and it was a good learning experience. I observed and assisted a public health nurse.

After this experience, Frances Cunningham had persuaded Mr. Ward, the hospital administrator, to employ two staff nurses beginning July 1937. Mary Lou Hicks and I were selected to work on A & B and C & D wards at $77.00 a month with board and laundry for a 52-hour week with one day off a month. Mary Lou and I were so happy to be offered these positions. There was an oversupply of nurses as hospitals employed their own graduates and students staffed all hospitals.

Marie Buckley in classroom

Marie Buckley's *account was based on a 1997 interview with Dr. Greenhill. Miss Buckley went on to earn her Baccalaureate in Nursing at Vanderbilt University and a master's degree in public health nursing at Teachers College, Columbia University. After teaching at the University of Texas, Galveston, and Vanderbilt University, she returned to the UT School of Nursing in August 1955 as Director of Clinical Instruction. ✦ At that time, no one on the faculty had a master's degree in a clinical specialty. Some of her efforts went to help each faculty member see the need to attend an accredited school of nursing and earn a master's degree in their chosen clinical specialty. ✦ She later served in numerous positions, including Director of Program for RN Students, Chairman of First Year Nursing and then Assistant Dean for Student Affairs. In 1968, she was awarded Goodman Professor for excellence in teaching. Marie Buckley retired in June 1980. ✦ In the 1997 interview, Miss Buckley stated: "I have often wondered why have UT graduates always received high preference in employment situations. I have talked to many directors of nursing services and a few chiefs of nursing in the armed services. I have finally come to the conclusion that it was due to our graduates having a high level of technical competence, extensive experience in caring for patients with a full range of diagnoses including the rare and unusual, and a great desire to be of service. Dean Murry was directly responsible for fostering these desirable attributes in our graduating students." ✦ EDITOR'S NOTE: Miss Buckley passed away in 2010 after the original publication of this history. ✦*

The World War II Years

The Angels of Bataan 1941-1945

BY E. DIANNE GREENHILL

"Angels of Bataan and Corregidor," "Angels of Mercy," and "The Unsung Heroines" are terms used to describe the Army and Navy nurses who were with our troops defending the Philippines during the early months of World War II. The Japanese began their attack on the Philippines on December 8, 1941, and by Christmas Eve had forced the retreat of American forces to the small peninsula of Bataan. The area was rugged and mountainous with swamps and dense jungle along the coast. The nurses set up field hospitals and endured countless hardships as they cared for the defenders. Bataan surrendered April 9, 1942 and 88 American and Filipino nurses transferred to the island fortress of Corregidor. Allied forces continued the battle until May 6, 1942 when General Wainwright surrendered all troops in the Philippine Islands. Fifty-six Army nurses on Corregidor were included in the surrender. Among this group, were two University of Tennessee graduates serving in the Army Nurse Corps.

Imogene Kennedy (Schmidt), 1945

Inez McDonald, a native of Plantersville, Mississippi (near Tupelo), graduated from the UT School of Nursing in December 1934. She joined the Army Nurse Corps in April 1937 after working at the Army & Navy Hospital in Hot Springs, Arkansas. Initially serving at Maxwell Field, Alabama, she was transferred to Ft. William McKinley near Manila in July 1941.

Imogene Kennedy came from a farming community near Philadelphia, Mississippi. She graduated from UT in September 1940. She had joined the Red Cross as a senior student agreeing to military service if called. After a brief experience at Methodist Hospital, she was called to reserve officer service in March 1941. Her first assignment was Ft. Benning, Georgia. In late October 1941, Lt. Kennedy traveled by an 18-day convoy to Manila. She also was assigned to Ft. McKinley when the attack came.

Life in the Philippines before the outbreak of war was described by the nurses as ideal, different from the depression conditions at home. The exotic locale provided many leisure activities such as golf, tennis, and horseback riding. The nurses also had comfortable living quarters with servants. Most of them did not seem to believe war would directly involve them.

The real hardships began when the evacuation to Bataan occurred. Two hospitals were set up in the jungle. Patients were in bamboo bunks and later on the ground under the trees. The operating room was a tent. Useless white uniforms were exchanged for men's coveralls. The nurses lived in canvas shelter halves and bathed and washed their clothes in the streams. Hospital supplies and food were in very short supply. Hunger was a major problem. Inez McDonald reported that the cavalry horses were useless against the

Japanese tanks so were used for food. The hospitals were frequently under attack. Hospital #1, also called "Little Baguio," was bombed twice; the second time was a direct hit on the wards where patients and two nurses were wounded. Lt. McDonald was quoted in *The Commercial Appeal* as follows: "The bomb came down on a hospital ward nearby. I lay flat on the floor of the ward, and while I was there, the bamboo and tar paper flew up into the air and came down all over me. I lay there for a few seconds. The air was full of dust and smoke." Inez also reported that in one night, she admitted 200 patients.

On April 8, 1942, the nurses were given 10 minutes to get ready to evacuate. They were transported under enemy fire by boat to Corregidor where they lived and worked in the Malinta Tunnel hospital. Although some nurses had been previously captured, none of those who were on Bataan were surrendered with the troops. The forced marches of American and Filipino troops contained no nurses.

The nurses felt safe in the deep tunnels of Corregidor, but the constant bombing brought noise, dust, and shaking. They stayed busy providing care for the many casualties. Imogene said they were allowed out of the tunnels about an hour twice a day — morning and evening. Most of them smoked. They did not have much to eat, but they had cigarettes. Corregidor fell on May 6, 1942. The nurses were held in the tunnels until June 25, 1942. They continued to care for their patients with meager supplies. They reused bloody gauze bandages after washing and sterilizing.

Eventually, they were transported to Santo Tomas, a university setting in Manila where they were imprisoned until the Philippine liberation. Sixty-seven Army nurses were held here with other civilian internees. There were about 5,000 men, women and children imprisoned at Santo Tomas. The nurses were separated from other military personnel and never suffered the severe depravity found in the military POW camps.

After a period of isolation, on August 25, 1942, the nurses were moved into the main civilian camp where they continued their struggle for survival for their almost three years of internment. Everyone in the internment camp had a job. The nurses set up a hospital and were scheduled on shifts. The senior nurse officer, Major Davidson, expected everyone to work unless they were sick.

Both Inez and Imogene shared memories of boredom, hunger and lack of privacy. However, in comparison with what they had experienced on Bataan and Corregidor, at least initially, it was better. They had to stand in lines to go to the bathroom, to get food, to do laundry, etc. One of the difficulties was not knowing about family and friends. Many of those at home did not know the fate of the nurses. Conditions worsened at the camp when in January 1944, the Japanese military assumed more control.

(top) Inez McDonald (right) with sister, Cadet Nurse Jimmie McDonald
(bottom) Inez McDonald (Moore)

Soldiers patrolled the grounds requiring everyone to bow. They were never physically mistreated but were in constant fear of their captors. There was less food as the Japanese themselves were receiving fewer supplies. Nurse historian Elizabeth Norman (1995) reports that by the end of 1944, the daily caloric intake was about 800 calories with no protein or fat. Finally they were liberated on February 3, 1945. Imogene wrote: "…the Americans rolled into the gates and liberated us — I've often wondered if the troops thought we were worth saving. We were a motley crew — everyone so dreadfully skinny and in tatters — but they were so good to us — gave us food and hope of seeing our families and homeland again."

Newspaper photo of Lts. Kennedy and McDonald taken on their arrival in San Francisco, 1945

The *Tupelo Daily Journal* on Tuesday morning, February 6, 1945, reported the joy of the McDonald family on knowing that their daughter was liberated. *The Commercial Appeal* also carried accounts and reported Imogene's cable to her mother that she "was well." Even though their long ordeal had ended, the nurses did not stop in their newly found work of caring for the wounded in the battle to free Manila. Newspaper accounts described their delight in having clean bandages and sufficient drugs including a new one, penicillin.

All of the "Angels" came home to a hero's welcome in the States. Each of the nurses, as Army prisoners of war, received the Bronze Star Medal and promotion of one grade. Both Inez and Imogene were honored with celebrations in their hometowns. *The Commercial Appeal* carried a full page feature story on Sunday, March 4, 1945.

After her return, Imogene married a Manila businessman, Richard J. Schmidt, who was a civilian POW at Santo Tomas. He was working in the hospital scrubbing floors. "He found out I was from Mississippi and he said, 'Hey Mississippi' I turned around and said 'Huh?' and the romance was on." They were at the same camp for one year when he was transferred to the Los Banos prison camp. They corresponded for two years and met again in Philadelphia, Mississippi, after her return home. Imogene was stationed at Oakland Regional Hospital until January 1946 when she separated from the Army.

Currently, Imogene and Dick live in California and have two children and four grand-children. When asked about memories of being hungry, Imogene stated: "Oh yes. Our cabinets are full of food now — I'll never go hungry again. I lost a lot of weight. My husband got beriberi."

Inez remained in the military becoming a part of the Air Force when that branch was established. She received her wings as an Air Force flight nurse in 1950. Her sister, Jimmie McDonald Wright (Class of June 1945) reports that Inez met her husband, Howard Moore, in the Air Force. Inez died of cancer May 1990 at Brooke Army Hospital.

How did the nurses survive the hardships? Part of the credit went to their nursing backgrounds and to the support and strength of their fellow nurses. Imogene reports her preparation at UT was important: "We had extremely superior training in nursing school — how to improvise, make do and eke out — which came in very handy in all the days of Bataan, Corregidor, and the prison camp." They persevered in difficult circumstances. UT is proud of our heroines of Bataan and World War II!

World War II Memories

BY JIMMIE MCDONALD WRIGHT,* BSN, CLASS OF 1945

I was in college on December 7, 1941, when Pearl Harbor was bombed and war was declared. I immediately applied to enter UT School of Nursing. I was accepted and entered UT Memphis July 1942. My dream had always been to follow in the foot prints of my sister who had graduated from UT at an earlier time. At that time, she was a second lieutenant In the Army Nurse Corps in Manila, Philippines.

The first three months of probation in Nursing are a testing and learning time in order to evaluate the ability to become a nurse. There were a few times when I wondered if I had made the correct choice. Fundamentals of nursing is where you learn the basic procedures and principles of nursing care. There were specific procedures written which had to be followed step by step. Making beds with the mitered corners was hard for me at first. The instructor kept taking her hand ripping out the corners. She taught me the procedure had to be followed as written. She taught me that determination was an attribute, which has carried me through many activities in my life.

One day I was in a treatment room performing my first catheterization on a patient. After a few steps, the instructor asked me, "What step have you missed?" My thought process went blank. She talked to me in a calm manner and calmed me down. I completed the procedure as it was written. Her discussion to me did not frighten the patient. Her calmness and confidence in me has helped me through many difficult situations. I also learned how to deal with students during my teaching career.

After completing the three-month probationary period successfully, we were given a UT Cap and the bib for our apron. Each of us were so proud and had love and respect for our instructors.

Shortage of supplies and personnel was always a problem. We were, at times, asked to do chores which did not relate to direct patient care. Some Saturday mornings we were assigned to clean the patient's bath room on each floor. The walls, commode, hopper and bed pans were cleaned.

We were also responsible for cleaning the bed and mattresses when a patient went home. We made the bed which would be ready for a new patient.

On the Wards, there were small kitchens with hot plates. Sometimes we were assigned to cook breakfast and serve the patients. This did not happen too often.

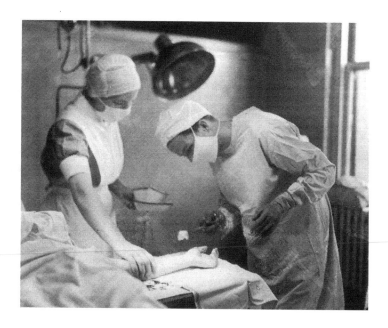

Jimmie McDonald assisting with procedure in 1944

Marcus Haase Residence around 1944, tennis courts in front

Since there was such a shortage of head Nurses, the Senior Nurses acted as Head Nurses on some of the Nursing Units. They were strict but usually fair because all of us were learning.

During this time we were to allow the Senior Nurses and Doctors to enter and leave elevators first. Many times I remember arriving at the dormitory door and waiting to hold the door open for the Senior Nurses. Since this was standard practice, we learned to respect these rules.

During our Junior and Senior years, our classes were taught by the Nursing Instructors and the Staff Doctors. The doctors taught the Anatomy and Physiology part of the subject and the Instructors taught the nursing content of procedures and the nursing principles. Even though we had to work the eight-hour shifts of 3-11 and 11-7, we were required to attend all classes. Many times it was very difficult to stay awake.

The Staff Doctors and Residents who were assigned to the Nursing Units would allow us to make rounds with them, help with dressing changes and learn from the discussions regarding patient care and treatment.

On the Pediatric Units, medical students were also assigned to the children. We learned together under the guidance of the Chief of Pediatrics and the Residents. Penicillin became available but only by injection. The injections were given in the buttocks and legs of the children every three hours which caused many local infections. Hot packs and holding the sick and crying children became a common thing we would do to try and comfort them. The Chief of Pediatrics was a great teacher and a caring doctor.

On the adult medical units, I remember how miserable the cardiac patients were because of their severe body edema. To help relieve their shortness of breath, they would sit on the side of the bed dangling their legs. Most had oxygen catheters in their noses and leaned their arms and head on the bedside table. We did not have medication to relieve the pulmonary edema. It was very difficult to make them comfortable. During the summer heat, without fans and air conditioning, the patients and the medical and nursing staff were even more uncomfortable.

My last six months of Nursing School, January - June 1945, were spent at Kennedy

General Military Hospital in Memphis as a Cadet Nurse. This was a government program designed to increase the number of military nurses. When I was assigned to Kennedy Hospital, my goal was to go into the Army Nurse Corp. In March 1945, my future husband was injured in France and was sent to Kennedy as a patient. We became friends and were married shortly after I graduated from UT in June. Needless to say that ended my thoughts of going into the military since married women were not allowed to join.

Even though we worked and studied hard during those three years, these were tough times due to shortages of supplies and personnel; however, we had our fun times. Everyone was very aware of the war and wanted to do our very best.

We could check out of the dormitory for movies downtown, to church, and other activities. We could visit friends in the community. Our mode of transportation was the electric street car for five cents. We also walked to nearby places. Anytime we checked out of the dormitory, we had to wear hats and gloves, especially if we went to church or downtown. I had played tennis at home and at college, so I was happy to have a tennis court near the dormitory.

My sister was liberated from the Japanese prison at Santo Tomas, Manila, Philippines on February 5, 1945. She flew to Memphis in March 1945. My parents and I met her at the airport. That was one the happiest days of my life to see her walking off the plane.

In July 1945 I was employed by John Gaston Hospital as a Night Supervisor, later as Head Nurse in Labor and Delivery. Two years after graduation, Miss Murry asked me to teach Pediatrics. Because of her confidence in me, I accepted the job. The principles of good nursing care and courage I had in accepting that position have sustained me throughout my nursing career. A few years ago I was asked to go to Indonesia and to India to assist the nurses and the physicians in devising programs of nursing principles and care. Without the experiences I gained as a student at UT, I would never have had the courage and determination to fulfill this request.

I am so proud to be a June 1945 graduate of The University of Tennessee. Thanks to all the Instructors, my classmates and many more who have made my nursing career so great.

Cadet Nurse McDonald, on right

*Jimmie McDonald Wright, *after graduating from UT in 1945, obtained a MEd in Guidance and Counseling. She has taught medical/surgical, pediatric and obstetrical nursing at UT and Baptist School of Nursing. ✦ She opened an Associate Degree Nursing Program at Itawamba Community College in Mississippi. Since retirement, she has served as a consultant in Jakarta, Indonesia and Delhi, India. She lives in Bartlett, Tennessee with her husband Raymond. ✦*

World War II Memories

BY VIRGINIA HARPER JONES,* BSN, CLASS OF 1945

The war, of course, was the thing that dominated and overshadowed and affected everything. I would not have been in nursing if I had not wanted to help out in the war effort.

The accelerated program brought in a new class every three months. There was a sense of urgency. The hospital was staffed mainly by students who took the places of RN's. It seemed that we started work on the wards almost at once. As soon as we learned to make beds we did so, and so on, throughout the three years. We used everything we learned almost immediately. It was a wonderful hands-on experience.

That first Christmas, most of us could not go home. On Christmas Eve, we gathered at midnight, dressed in our starched student uniforms and caps. We were each given a lighted candle, and we walked through the darkened wards carrying the candle and singing carols.

There was a chronic shortage of supplies such as linens. Somehow, supplies would suddenly appear just before an election in (E.H.) Crump dominated Memphis.

Virginia Harper (on right) with classmate in 1944 at Forrest Park

Students rotated shifts, working a month on each shift. I was on night duty one summer. We had a sort of dorm with bunk beds on the first floor for students on the night shift. No air conditioning, of course; only the OR was air conditioned. We were so miserably hot that we could not sleep. We would wet our sheets and wrap ourselves in them in an effort to get cool. No matter what hours we were working, we had to get up and attend our classes during the day. I lost 10 lb. every month I was on night duty.

During the polio epidemic, John Gaston was one of the few hospitals that employed the Sister Kenny method of treatment. In fact, Sister Kenny came to Memphis during that time. We had a whole ward full of iron lungs. There were also patients in the acute infectious stage of the disease. We learned strict aseptic technique. There were no antibiotics. The Kenny treatment was

***Virginia Harper Jones,** after graduating from UT in 1945, worked as a staff nurse and Director of Nursing in Oak Ridge, Tennessee until 1949. ✦ She served as a public health nurse in Winston-Salem, North Carolina, and taught at Forsyth Memorial Hospital School of Nursing from 1964 until her retirement in 1974. She lives in Winston-Salem with her husband Henry. ✦

aimed at preventing paralysis by applying very hot wool wraps to the affected limbs. The strips of heavy army blankets were wrung (with a hand-wringer washing machine) out of almost boiling water and applied.

After my first year, I dropped out to marry my college sweetheart, Robert Lee Brown. He soon went overseas. I applied to Miss Murry for readmission. At that time, there was a strict rule against married students. Miss Murry went to the "Powers-That-Be," and they changed the rule. After that, many other married students were admitted.

I feel that my years at UT were a great experience. It gave me confidence that made me not afraid to tackle anything! I am even grateful to Miss Murry and the teachers for what they gave me.

World War II Memories

BY VERNON TOWNSLEY HARGETT,* BSN, CLASS OF 1945

During the years from 1942-1945, everyone was feeling very patriotic, and felt we needed to serve our country during this stressful period. Since nurses were desperately needed, I felt the time had come for me to fulfill my heart's desire and become the nurse I had always wanted to be. Our class started with 33 girls, and only nine graduated due to many reasons. To me, those nine were the "cream of the crop."

While at UT, I tried to begin a Student Government Program patterned after the one I participated in at the University of Alabama before coming to UT. I am not sure how worthwhile it was, or if it lasted after I left, but I tried.

A few tidbits I recall about some experiences while in training may only be of interest to me, but I will pass them on for what they are worth. Night duty was never a favorite shift for me, but it had to be done. While working one night (I think it was on pediatrics), we girls got so hungry between supper and breakfast that we made coffee and had some snacks on the sly. Naturally we got caught! We argued our case, as gracefully as we could, and before long we were provided food in the ward kitchens. We were very grateful.

Once in Miss Murry's obstetrics class, first of the morning after night duty, she must have caught some of us dozing. Without calling any

Vernon Townsley (second from left, second row) with classmates shopping in downtown Memphis in 1943

names, she made it very clear and emphatic, that we were not to sleep in her class, even if we had just come off night duty. I felt guilty because my notes started on one line and ended several lines below. I do not think I was alone. Even so, I loved and respected her.

While preparing a surgical dressing tray under the watchful eye of Miss Ann Messerly, our Surgical Supervisor, I was so nervous I think I was shaking. Without a word, she left me at that time. I was so disappointed because I was anxious to get that procedure checked off in my procedure notebook. During lunch in the cafeteria, she came to me and asked for my book. She checked it for me. I could have hugged her at that moment, even though a short while ago I was terrified. Following graduation, we became friends.

Psychiatry promised another unwelcomed experience for me. While going on duty one morning, I was on the elevator with my supervisor. He looked at me, and told me to remove my lipstick even though I was wearing the very pale Tangee that was prevalent at that time. That was no excuse. She did not permit make-up while on duty.

One of the nicest surprises I received near the end of my training was being awarded the Trustee's Medal for service. I did not feel worthy, but I considered it a great honor and much appreciated.

There were some sad times while at UT

U.S. Cadet Nurse uniform insignia

involving two of my former roommates. Virginia Harper Jones received news one day that her husband, who was in the service, was reported missing in action. Needless to say, we were devastated. We continued to hope and pray that he would be found, but he was not until much later. The family was told he had been killed in action and was buried in Italy.

The second tragedy involved Jimmie McDonald Wright. Her sister, Inez McDonald, was held prisoner while in the Philippines. Fortunately, she did return after quite a while, but the pain was very evident to all of us until she did.

The Cadet Nurse Corps was established by Uncle Sam to interest student nurses to enter the Armed Services. We made a commitment to join if we were able. I thought my plans were made also, but since there were so few nurses on staff to keep the School of Nursing and John Gaston Hospital going, Miss Murry had me reclassified as "essential to the school." I do not know why she chose me because I had never been a teacher. I was appointed to be the Medical Supervisor and teach Medical Nursing and Dermatology. What an experience that was! However, the girls were very nice, and we made it through together.

Attending UT and working there after graduation was a genuine pleasure and learning experience. The education was invaluable, and the friends were everlasting.

---

*Vernon Townsley Hargett *received a BEd from the University of Alabama before entering nursing at UT.* ✦ *She worked as a supervisor in medical nursing before retiring to care for her husband and three children. She lives in Alabama with her family.* ✦

Decade of the 1950s

BY CAROLYN DePALMA,* BSN, CLASS OF 1956

The 1950's found us in the middle of a century marked by progress and ideas that were only a dream 50 years before at the turn of the century. At the University of Tennessee School of Nursing in the Fifties, we were mostly female, between the ages of 17 and 35 (according to the admission criterion), and mostly unmarried. Our parents came to adulthood in the Twenties or Thirties, and our grandmothers could not vote for the President of the United States.

We were profoundly influenced by our big sisters and brothers, who in the decade before, had either served in the armed forces or helped on the home front to successfully win the Second World War. When we arrived on the campus of the University of Tennessee in Memphis, many of our instructors in nursing were veterans of the Navy or Army Nurse Corps. All but two students were female. Charles Wilson Yoakum of Memphis was the first man who graduated from the School of Nursing. James Macdonald Hunn of Arkansas was the second man to graduate from the School of Nursing in December 1956. Both men exemplified the highest standards in their professionalism.

The prospective student was introduced to the school and campus at a required two-day orientation at which time tests were administered. One met for the first time classmates with whom one might spend the next three or four years of their lives. Students stayed in the Marcus Haase Dormitory for the sum of one dollar for two days and ate in the hospital cafeteria for 50 cents per meal. If accepted into the program, the student deposited $10, which was taken off the first quarter fees.

The course of study was rigorous for all students. Students who were to obtain a certificate began their study with Nursing Arts, and very shortly began working on the wards giving care to patients. The four-year students

Carolyn Moran (DePalma), far right, with classmates in front of Marcus Haase

began Nursing Arts in the fourth quarter with morning or afternoon care and then progressed through the curriculum of Nursing Arts. By the sixth quarter, the student was either in Medical Nursing or Surgical Nursing and assigned to the appropriate ward for each area. Ward M&O was often used for beginning students so that skills could be applied early, for the patients on this ward were not as ill. The students were on the ward to give evening care under the guidance of their instructors.

The instructors in the Nursing Arts program

(left) "The Bedpan Lament" Skit at UT Student Center. Students – Barbara Allen, Carolyn (Dixie) Moran (DePalma), and Virginia Threlkeld
(right) Gailor Psychiatric Hospital

have a capping ceremony, and they received their caps in a shortened version of the common capping ceremony of the day. Senior students received a black band for their caps. Black bands were awarded in a banding ceremony. The class behind the black banded class had a special supper set up in the cafeteria to mark this rite of passage. It was a moment of pride to have achieved senior status.

were awe inspiring to the students, for they had an air of quiet confidence that demanded the students' best. Miss Wellman was one such instructor from those years, and with her quiet voice and her professional air, she inspired the students to learn the best possible care. The instructors were impeccably groomed and wore long-sleeved, white uniforms that remained unwrinkled after assisting students with their care. Students' uniforms were of white cotton, stiffly starched, short sleeved dress with an orange patch on the left sleeve identifying them as a UT Student. The cap worn was the official Red Cross Cap. The men wore white pants and a tunic with the orange seal on the sleeve. White stockings and shoes were worn with the woman's uniform. The cape to be worn on cold days was mid-thigh length of navy wool with a red wool lining. The Mandarin collar had UT in gold embroidery. If a sweater was worn, it had to be white.

In many diploma schools of this era, the cap was sacrosanct and given to young students after a probationary period on the wards. A UT cap was considered part of the uniform, but capping ceremonies were not encouraged, for Dean Murry, it was said, did not believe in them. Some classes, however persuaded her to allow them to

Following the quarters of Nursing Arts, students began working evening shifts, 3 p.m. to 11 p.m. and then were in charge of a ward. Our wards were built to hold 40 patients in two large rooms that held 20 beds each. The beds were iron and had an over bed table and nightstand. When treatments demanded privacy, portable screens were used. Often however, due to overflow and the critical needs of patients, cots were brought up and patients were assigned to cots placed in the middle of the wards or in the hall. I can recall a census of 61 on T&W, a ward for men. The hospital was still using a 44-hour work week until July of 1955, and students worked within that framework. However, class hours were subtracted from hospital work hours.

John Gaston Hospital, the site of our practice, was a city hospital and supplies were not plentiful. It was frustrating not to have the necessary items needed for our patients' comfort. Most of our patients were quite ill with multiple diagnoses. Antibiotics included penicillin and streptomycin, terramycin, chloromycetin, and a few others, but all of these treatments were still quite new in the Fifties. All surgery patients received prophylactic antibiotics that would necessitate 30-40 intramuscular injections. On

FROM DIPLOMA TO DOCTORATE:

the medical wards, patients with peptic ulcers received half-hour feedings of cream that were alternated with an antacid. This patient might also receive tincture of belladonna. The emergency treatment for patients with pulmonary edema as a result of congestive heart failure included rotating tourniquets and numerous medications. Cardiovascular status was assessed with pulse and blood pressure monitoring.

Among the communicable diseases encountered were typhoid fever, tuberculosis and poliomyelitis. Infants with pertussis were quite common on pediatrics. Isolation procedure was formidable and required much necessary time to protect oneself and others. Drugs and the Salk vaccine would soon eradicate many of these diseases.

During the '50's, the Dean still served in loco parentis for the young women entrusted to her care. Time away from the dormitory was carefully monitored. This monitoring resulted in "Signing-out." During the first quarters of schooling, students were limited to one eleven o'clock outing per week. Even those who went on weekends with parents of students who lived in Memphis had to be given permission by the Dean or her Assistant, Mrs. Grace Wallace, to leave campus. For a weekend away to a Baptist Student Union Convention in Johnson City, the father of one young woman wrote, "I give permission, if Miss Wallace approves."

Students lived in Marcus Haase dormitory, which was in the back of the hospital, and took meals in the cafeteria of the John Gaston Hospital. The right to have an apartment off campus occurred in the later part of the Fifties. Until that time, students lived in the dorm. The exception to this was the students who married.

For students did marry while in school, with the permission of the Dean. After a personal interview was conducted, permission was granted. In the class of 1956, two-thirds of the graduates who received their degrees were married.

Nursing in the Fifties was a time of profound change, but little could we have anticipated the Sixties and the changes that would occur. We were prepared however, in one sense, for if we learned one lesson above others, it was to adapt and be prepared. Our educational experiences were based not on rote learning, but understanding the under lying rationale for care. We knew that we were excellent nurses, but it would be in later years that we would fully appreciate what a visionary Dean Murry was, and although curriculum is the province of faculty, she was the leader. We graduated believing that a UT graduate could function well in whatever nursing circumstance she found herself.

Student party scene in the early 1950s

Carolyn Moran DePalma graduated from UT in December 1956 and worked as staff nurse, head nurse and supervisor at John Gaston Hospital. She received her MA from Teachers College, Columbia and has taught in various colleges. ♦ She has course work toward a doctorate at the University of Cincinnati. "Dixie" and her husband have retired in St. Augustine, Florida. ♦

Decade of the 1960s

BY MARGARET A. NEWMAN,* BSN, CLASS OF 1962

My decision to enroll in the University of Tennessee College of Nursing in Memphis in the fall of 1959 occurred after a long inner struggle with a "calling" to become a nurse. A year before, I had explored that possibility with Grace Wallace and had told her that my primary interest was in understanding more about illness, but I was not sure I wanted to do anything about it. She replied that maybe I should go into Medicine rather than Nursing! But the lingering call to nursing continued; so immediately after my mother's death following a long illness, and in spite of my strong disinclination to enter a career in nursing, I took steps to enter the baccalaureate program in nursing at UT. (Incidentally, Grace Wallace told me in retrospect that she did not think she would ever see me again.)

Those first days in Louise Rapp's fundamentals class were exhilarating. Suddenly I could see that the focus of nursing was on understanding the human experience of health and illness, and that it would require the best I had to offer. An added bonus was something I had not thought about and did not expect — my relationship with members of the class of 1962. My classmates were intelligent, personable women who clearly had a commitment to serve others. I had a sense of camaraderie that I had not experienced before in my previous college days. I was part of something bigger than myself.

It is hard to remember the specifics of my learning through the various clinical experiences, but one of my early encounters with patients on a medical unit (G&H) stands out. I was assigned to care for a teenage girl

Margaret Newman,
nursing student in 1961

who had juvenile diabetes and had been admitted in a coma, an event that was not new to her. She was bright and attractive and understood on some level what was going on, but she did not heed the medical instructions for her care. I remember the physician yelling at her and telling her she was going to die. That made little impression on her. I had gathered all the information that I thought was relevant: psychological, sociological, and of course, medical. But I still did not know what to do. I shared my confusion with my instructor Dorothy Hocker, and she, within an instant of interaction with the patient, got in sync with this young girl and grasped the patients' perspective on the situation. It was hard to explain, then and now, but I knew there was a connecting with the person, and I had been a part of it, and it had made a difference. I knew that the knowledge

to define criteria we would use in selecting a graduate program for further study in nursing, and I was well on my way to pursuing the knowledge of the discipline. About the same time, Dean Ruth Neil Murry, a truly visionary nurse, encouraged us to formulate the questions we wanted to answer in the form of research and arranged for an expert from the Division of Nursing to assist us in making those proposals a reality.

The friendships with classmates and the faculty mentors formed at the University of Tennessee College of Nursing have continued to guide and strengthen me throughout my career. During graduate study at other universities, I was well aware of the strength of my educational foundations at UTCN, and as I look back, it is clear that my theoretical roots stem from UT as well. Now, as my papers are being collected at the University of Tennessee Health Sciences Library and will be available for exploration by future nurse scholars, I feel as though I have come full circle. I am pleased to be back at UT.

of nursing was not the summing up of all that information I had collected, but a connecting person with person. I did not know it then, but I was on my way to a career of trying to explicate the discipline of nursing.

When I was a senior, Marie Buckley reinforced that budding idea that nursing had a knowledge and practice of its own by suggesting that some nurses were beginning to "hang out their shingles," a truly revolutionary and exciting idea at the time. She also helped us

*(left) Going to convention
(above) Dr. Margaret Newman,
Professor Emeritus, University
of Minnesota*

__Margaret Ann Newman__ was asked to submit this article describing the influence of the College of Nursing on her development as a nursing theorist. Her nursing papers have been donated to The University of Tennessee, Memphis Library. ✦ Margaret Ann Newman received a bachelor's degree from Baylor University prior to attending UT Memphis. After receiving her BSN in 1962, she earned a master's degree in medical-surgical nursing from the University of California, San Francisco and her PhD in nursing science and rehabilitation nursing from New York University in 1971. ✦ She has taught at UT Memphis, New York University and Pennsylvania State University. She was a professor at the University of Minnesota prior to her recent retirement. She is known internationally for her Theory of Health as expanding consciousness. She has published four books, numerous articles and book chapters. ✦

Decade of the 1960s

BY JEANETTE LANCASTER,* BSN, CLASS OF 1966

As I look back to those intense three years when 29 of us entered The University of Tennessee College of Nursing with great anticipation about becoming nurses, it is hard to know where to begin and what to include. Because there were only 29 of us, we somehow knew we had been carefully chosen. Each of us had been a good student in high school and now we set out to learn our profession amidst a group of capable peers.

Dr. Jeannette Lancaster
Dean
School of Nursing
University of Virginia

Interestingly, given our keen interest in becoming nurses, the rigors of a baccalaureate curriculum delivered in three years, and the competence of our class, I do not think back and remember competition. Rather there was camaraderie, helpfulness and assistance. We never thought any of us would succeed at the expense of another. Some of us, perhaps especially me, wondered if I would succeed, but I had great confidence that my classmates would be successful. Our course work at the then Memphis State University was much like the work we had each done in the first two years of our college education, and we dutifully drove across town to take such things as philosophy and sociology. The science courses at UT were fraught with interesting stories. Just my luck, the chemistry teacher that I had in my freshman year at Arkansas State was now at UT Memphis. Despite his kind smile and patience, I was unable to "bond" with chemistry, though I did start a small fire with my Bunsen burner. Who would have thought that shoving the burner back under the storage shelf while it was still ignited would cause such an uproar!

And then we got to the NURSING COURSES. The faculty were as different from one another as could be imagined. They ranged from patient and laid back to tense and insistent in their desire for us to learn. All were competent and knew their area of specialty. They just had individualized styles for inspiring us to want to learn, to grow, to "be all you can be."

Our clinical sites and experiences were as varied as our faculty. We went from the expert care and tranquility at St. Jude to the hustle and bustle of John Gaston. We learned from the nurses and physicians at St. Jude to deal with sick and terminally ill children and their families in an atmosphere of caring, compassion, and communication about what was happening and what could be expected to happen. At John Gaston, we worked with a variety of patients, many of whom were indigent and had few supports and resources outside the hospital. The pace was fast and the staff was small and seemed to rely on our assistance. Our community health and psychiatric nursing experiences were rich ones taught by thoughtful, capable faculty and in agencies that were able to provide comprehensive care. In those days, it was safe to walk through alleys in Memphis to make home visits to clients who lived on lanes not roads. The clients and their neighbors were glad to see us, and they believed we had something besides kindness to offer them.

Throughout the curriculum and in each clinical experience, we were taught to think, plan and provide care that would make a difference, whether it was at home or in the hospital or clinic. We were "prodded" not "coddled" so that we would continually reach higher and grow stronger in our knowledge and skills.

As the years have gone by, I have become

more grateful for the exacting standards of the faculty at UT. In those years of nursing school, I often thought that I would just never learn to be a nurse; that I would just never measure up. However, as I have moved from clinician in psychiatric nursing to faculty member, to program director, and more finally, to dean, I have come to appreciate more fully the benefits of high standards. As I teach students in the undergraduate program at the University of Virginia and as I read the current writings in organizational development, I realize that holding people to high standards is a good, early lesson in how to become a desirable employee. What we know today is that the employees of both the present and the futures must be nimble, adaptable, willing to commit fully to the organization, work as though they owned the organization, create solutions to problems rather than either being a problem or creating a series of them, and engage in life-long learning so they continually refocus and replenish what they know. We learned many of these skills in our undergraduate program. We also learned to gather and organize information, to write and to speak, to prioritize and strategize; and we learned to know which rules could be bent and which were like steel rods and must be acknowledged and accepted as they were.

I was especially drawn to psychiatric nursing and public health nursing. In both specialty areas, I believed that nursing care could make a

(top) View of Medical Center in early 1960's
(bottom) Student-faculty tea in mid 60's

*Jeanette Lancaster *was asked to submit this article describing the influence of the College of Nursing on her development as a leader in nursing education.* ✦ *Jeanette Lancaster received her BSN from UT in 1966, her MS in psychiatric mental health nursing from Case Western Reserve University, and her PhD in public health from the University of Oklahoma.* ✦ *She has served as Dean and Professor at Wright State University in Dayton, Ohio, and has been Dean and Sadie Heath Cabaniss Professor of Nursing at the University of Virginia since 1989. She has edited or co-edited four nursing text books including* Community Health Nursing: Processes and Practices for Promoting Health. ✦

difference. The faculty team in each course was without exception comprised of capable women who, while holding students to high standards of performance, conveyed genuine liking and respect for the students. They believed we could learn and ultimately make a contribution to health care.

As I look at the huge changes that have occurred in health care and the changing role expectations of nurses, I am grateful for the foundation in nursing that was built at UT Memphis and upon which I later added graduate study and a lifelong career in nursing.

Decade of the 1960s

BY CHERYL CUMMINGS STEGBAUER,* BSN, CLASS OF 1969

Health care in the 1960's was vastly different. At that time hepatitis was classified as "infectious" or "noninfectious." Gloves were not worn to start an IV or to draw blood, and needles were always recapped after use as a "safety" measure. HIV was unknown. Oral contraceptives came on the market (in very large doses). The "Lamaze" method of natural childbirth was just being introduced to Memphis, and most hospitals did not allow fathers in the delivery room. Mammography, MRIs, CAT Scans, and ultrasound were not available as diagnostic tools. Loretta Ford and Henry Silver opened the first Nurse Practitioner program in Colorado, and education for registered nurses in Tennessee still was rooted strongly in diploma schools.

In the 1960's, The University of Tennessee, Memphis was the only nursing program in the UT system, and the College of Nursing enrolled students from across Tennessee as well as from the surrounding states. Benlyn Dezonia, Florence Petree, Nancey Underwood, and I, along with two RN students, Peggy Varnell and Britt Finley were the only entering students who were from Memphis out of a class of approximately 50. The majority of the class of 1969 entered as young 19 and 20-year-old women after completing pre-nursing courses in sciences and liberal arts. As students, we soon were given the privilege and challenge of learning to provide nursing care for other human beings in some of the most difficult and complex situations.

All graduates are a reflection of the time and of the broader society in which they live.

The decade of the 60's was a time of rapid social change that shaped our experiences as students in the College of Nursing. By the late 1960's, the country was engaged fully in the Vietnam War. While students on the West Coast protested the war, my class of 1969 provided nursing care to soldiers who were wounded in Vietnam. The Veterans Administration Hospital in Memphis had moved from the old Kennedy Complex at Park and Getwell to a new facility at Poplar and Pauline in the medical center. The new hospital had a state of the art unit for veterans with spinal cord injury. It was there that we learned about the tragedy of war and the hope of rehabilitation. It was the first time many of us had to face the reality that our youth did not mean being invincible as we helped young men our own age learn to perform activities of daily living in view

of life-altering spinal cord injuries. I remember one young man who told of lying wounded in the field and then being aware of losing feeling and movement in his arms and legs when he was lifted from the ground to a hovering helicopter. Such accounts were common.

One of the most interesting lectures I remember was on triage and was taught by Captain Elinor Reed. Elinor was one of our faculty members and served as Chief Nurse of the 155th Aeromedical Evacuation Flight with the Tennessee Air National Guard. Dean Ruth Neil Murry had given Elinor a leave of absence to participate in the air evacuation of American soldiers who had been wounded in Vietnam; she requested and served the maximum 89-day tour of active duty. She was based at Hickam Air Force Base, Honolulu, Hawaii. The air evacuation flights were staged primarily out of Yokota, Japan and Clark Air Base in the Philippines. While on one of the flights, she was talking to a young, wounded Marine who was being evacuated. During the course of conversation, Elinor learned that he too was from Tennessee and was the husband of one of her UT students.

It also was during a clinical rotation at

Veterans Hospital that many in my class first learned of the assassination of Dr. Martin Luther King, Jr., who had come to Memphis in support of the sanitation worker's strike. We were given the news of this tragic event by our clinical instructor. It was late afternoon, and we were told to leave the hospital immediately because the city was being placed under curfew. The curfew continued as National Guard troops patrolled the streets of Memphis, and tanks and soldiers were positioned on Main Street to prevent looting or violence. Some of the students who lived in high-rise apartments in the Medical Center told about looking out their windows and seeing the fires that had been set in surrounding neighborhoods. Staff at John Gaston Hospital, Crump Women's Hospital, Tobey Children's Hospital, and Gailor Outpatient Clinics largely were responsible for the health care of the city's indigent population, and some workers (including some nurses) at those City of Memphis facilities were striking along with city sanitation workers.

These facilities provided major clinical sites for UT students. In Marie Buckley's class, we debated and explored the issues of whether nurses should strike and what we believed to

(left) Dr. Cheryl Cummings Stegbauer, Associate Professor, University of Tennessee, Memphis College of Nursing (below) Captain Elinor F. Reed receiving the Tennessee Distinguished Service Award from Gov. Buford Ellington in 1967 in recognition of her service in Southeast Asia.

Nursing student uniforms 1920's-1968

clinical experiences in community health agencies and in both private and publicly funded hospitals. Those experiences involving such diverse settings and populations contributed to our view of what it means to see the patient as a whole, in the context of environment, and to our view of nurse as patient advocate.

During our senior year, we had year-long, concurrent classes and clinical rotations in obstetrics, community health, and psychiatric nursing. This allowed students to integrate concepts across clinical areas and to obtain depth through experience. The work of Hildegard Peplau provided a theoretical basis for psychiatric nursing and an introduction to an early nurse theorist. Students completed projects that focused on prevention and instilled the view that intervening to prevent illness was a nursing role. Statistics was a required course (my first introduction to the Framingham Study was in our statistics course that was taught by Dr. Eugene Fowinkle, Medical Director of the Memphis and Shelby County Health Department). All students carried out a clinical study as a requirement in a class taught by Marie Buckley and Dr. Ted May, from the College of Medicine. We were introduced to early nursing research as a basis for practice including some of the work at that time on the benefits of preoperative teaching.

My classmates were, and still are, the cream of the crop. Admission to the UT College of Nursing was very competitive, and that perhaps explains the story my mother recently told me. My mother had accompanied me to the college

be appropriate professional roles and responsibilities at such a time. Marie took a poll of our class and only two students did not support nurses striking. As students, we followed our patients as they were moved from the city facilities, and care was shifted to private hospitals in the community.

There were many aspects of the nursing curriculum that were outstanding. We had the advantage of having classes taught by faculty from other colleges on campus as well as from nursing. We had courses in Child Psychology, Adolescent Psychology, and Anthropology that were taught by College of Medicine faculty including Dr. Allen Battle (a professor my class held in high esteem). There was a wealth of

*Cheryl Cummings Stegbauer graduated from UT in 1969, received her MS in nursing at Texas Woman's University, Houston in 1974 and her PhD with a major in Nursing at UT Memphis in 1994. ✦ While living in Houston, she worked as a family nurse clinician in the Department of Community Medicine, Baylor College of Medicine. ✦ She is a tenured Associate Professor of Nursing at UT Memphis where she is engaged in primary care practice, teaching of both master's and doctoral students, and clinical research. ✦

FROM DIPLOMA TO DOCTORATE:

for my admission interview. She knew how much I wanted to be a nurse and said a silent prayer for me while I was in my interview with Grace Wallace. I certainly believe that prayers work, especially those from our mothers; however, when it came to being admitted to the College of Nursing, it did not hurt to have a few good words from Grace Wallace. To this day, I remember my response to one of Grace's questions. I told her that if I could not be a nurse, I did not think I could ever walk into a hospital without feeling regret. To that, Grace replied, "anyone who feels that strongly about nursing should have the opportunity."

Decade of the 1960s

BY VIRGINIA TROTTER BETTS,* BSN, CLASS OF 1969

*I*n the Fall of 1966, I came to the UT College of Nursing not on a mission but on an exploration. I really had no great calling or ambition to become a nurse – there were already several of us in my family – but I had been very interested in my biology and zoology courses at UT Knoxville and thought one year in Memphis (much farther away from my omnipresent parents in Sevierville) casually studying nursing as applied biology might be a lark. The lark idea was spoiled during my very first encounter with Mary Morris, et al; and I fully intended to head off to another school and another major at Christmas break. Somehow, due to great friends and some classroom times that challenged my intellectual curiosity, I just never got around to applying elsewhere and transferring, and am I glad!!

I have now been a professional nurse for almost 30 years, and I have loved all the varied career paths I have experienced. Since graduation so long ago, I have been a staff nurse, a hospital-based clinical specialist, a community mental health program director, a nurse educator, an association leader, and a health policy activist. As I review my career (as I have been asked to do for this publication), I know that I was inspired to fulfill, and prepared for succeeding at, many of these roles as a University of Tennessee graduate – a professional nurse.

I hope it is neither my age nor my nostalgia for the 100th anniversary of the UT College of Nursing (need I say Memphis?) to point out that educating a nurse to become a professional is not what it used to be — at least like it was

to a member of the Class of '69. While sitting there in those very cramped quarters, listening (rare for me and my close friends, or so the faculty thought!) to lectures and discussions that were frequently boring (a list of what a patient should pack to take to the hospital? Ugh!) but sometimes inspiring, or while putting in clinical hours at Gaston, Tobey, or Shelby County Public Health, I am sure that I heard a clear message. I heard that I — one professional nurse — could indeed make a difference that was needed, important, and significant, and that I had better learn the knowledge, skills, and personal attributes that would be required to make that difference.

Thus, UT gave me not only the credentials and knowledge to be a successful practicing

Virginia Trotter Betts

nurse, but also the following fundamental, abiding value precepts: (1) that health care is a right; (2) that nurses must be involved in securing that right for all persons; (3) that nurses are essential providers in a well functioning delivery system; and (4) that nurses must seek their own professional destiny.

I graduated believing that planned social change was possible, necessary, and a part of my repertoire and responsibility as a nurse. From the time of graduation to now, I have been working on making a difference in health care and for nursing, although my ideas, approaches, and scope have changed with time, maturity, and opportunity. As with most nurses, my focus for positive interventions began at the patient and facility level, and after graduate school, I refocused on community and population-based care. Career roles then allowed and influenced me to focus on change and growth within the profession of nursing, and then (and now) toward reforming and reshaping the health care delivery system through changes in its public policy.

I believe that a sound education is a funda-

mental prerequisite to achievement, and that a sound education in nursing is a complex mix of curriculum, teaching and clinical practice. On so many occasions, I have paused and reflected with admiration on these aspects of my BSN education at UT.

First the curriculum (for most, a length of five years) allowed a full year examination of the major clinical areas in professional nursing practice. That full year of content and clinical practice (even though the settings rotated) allowed a mastery of nursing far beyond initial "new graduate" competence. How else could Pam Morris and I (after just completing our junior year) have managed to successfully serve as COSTEP nurses in a USPHS hospital experiencing labor unrest for a whole summer without incident? Every day, we were thankful to have had such a *thorough* course in both med-surg and peds which gave us both the knowledge and the confidence that we **could do** the assigned care and do it competently without experienced RNs at our side. The curriculum at UT at the time allowed **true immersion** in clinical topics plus a choice of opportunities for clinical practice that so surpassed what graduates from other schools of nursing had experienced that I was frequently able to say, "been there, done that," when I arrived for graduate school which in turn gave me extensive flexibility for enhanced master's studies.

Yet no curriculum, no matter how well crafted, can launch its recipients without critical faculty interaction and leadership. I can still recall numerous thrilling "Ahhaa" experiences in the classroom and clinical conferences when I "got it," and an important bit of nursing was passed on. I remember clearly many of my school-day patients and their particular problems which I worked to solve. I also remember one faculty's clinical evaluation of me that included the statement, "Performs best with difficult or exceptional cases rather than the more routine." *That* gives me hope that I could return to today's clinical arena where all inpatient cases are both difficult and exceptional or else they would not be there! (By the way, I also remember who wrote that!)

I could list a whole variety of exceptional faculty and exquisite learning moments with them when they shaped my thinking, performance, and commitments in a most extraordinary way. However, I think that the greatest contribution that the faculty of the College of Nursing made on shaping my career was not as much *what they said* about nursing and health care but *what they did* and the *expectations* they projected. So many of the faculty held leadership positions in professional and health care organizations and, rather than just teach about professionalism and activism, they lived it!! (Just consider Dean Murry and Dorothy Hocker and their impact on the Tennessee Nurses Association.) Likewise, as students we were all encouraged to be members of the Tennessee Association of Student Nurses, and the only test I was ever allowed to make up without an act of God was one I missed serving as a TASN officer. Therefore, it **never** occurred to me that I could ever be a true professional nurse *unless* I was active in professional associations.

ANA/TNA/APHA/TPHA/NLN (to name a few) were presented as essential forces for good in the profession and in health care and were one direct method for nurses to achieve their goals and aims. While I am now aware that some in the Class of '69 did not take the professional association message to heart as intensively as I did, I know that they must at least feel **guilty** if they do not belong to some group that advances nursing and health care. It was simply *expected* and *modeled* by the College faculty.

Clinical practice opportunities at UT were

exceptional both in variety and in expectations for student performance. We cared for patients with great variance in economic means and education and with both the newest and the most antiquated equipment. We used public and private institutions, and we provided both illness and wellness care. Our clinicals and clinical conferences were used to push, pull, and pound us into **professional** nurses, and our clinical faculty plus the staff of each agency in which we practiced gave us the feeling of total responsibility for our patient's care, record keeping, and utilization of community resources. Additionally, as we discovered gaps in care delivery, we were expected to suggest to key staff possible options for delivery system improvement. What a heady experience for a neophyte, yet what an educational message:

Virginia Trotter Betts, President of the American Nurses Association, featured on the Spring 1993 issue of Tennessee Nurse

"Nurses and their ideas for positive change are important! You can and you must speak up."

Writing this chapter has allowed me to look back and ask myself some "cause and effect" questions such as: Without my reverence for Dean Murry, would I have ever sought the Tennessee Nurses Association then the American Nurses Association presidency — the greatest leadership opportunity for any nurse? Without my respect for Norma Long, would I have pursued both MSN and JD — degrees that led directly to my many opportunities to be involved in health policy development? Without close association with Mary Ann Barbee, would I have chosen Psych-Mental Health for my specialty — an essential background for understanding others during times of great anxiety and change? Without Stokes, Wallace, Greenhill, Morris, and Buckley, would I have ever *really known*

just how important compassion can be — for, without theirs, I would not have been a nurse? Without Cheryl, Jackie, Brenda, Dianne, Pam, Bonnie and all my classmates in the Class of '69, would I have survived and then thrived?

Not likely!

Armed with cutting-edge knowledge, a passion for nursing, and a self concept that encouraged risk taking, I left the College of Nursing and have practiced at those overt and covert lessons of professionalism ever since. In June 1969, I would never have believed or even imagined the highs, the lows, the joys, and the anxieties of my nursing career; yet I was prepared — prepared to work hard, to do well by doing good, to value myself, my colleagues, and my profession, and most importantly, in the midst of all this serious "stuff," to always have fun. I learned all of that at the UT College of Nursing — Thanks!

---

*Virginia Trotter Betts was asked to submit this article describing the influence of the College of Nursing on her development as a past president of the American Nurses Association and a nursing leader in health policy. After graduation from UT in 1969, she earned a MSN at Vanderbilt University and a JD from Nashville School of Law. ✦ Honors and distinctions include: Robert Wood Johnson Health Policy Fellowship; American Political Science Association Congressional Fellowship; Special White House Delegate to the 46th and 49th World Health Assemblies; US Delegate to the Fourth World Conference on Women in Beijing. She was president of the American Nurses Association from 1992-1996. ✦ In December 1997, she was appointed Senior Advisor on Nursing Policy to the Secretary of Health and Human Services and Senior Advisor to the Assistant of Public Health and Science. ✦

Decade of the 1970s

BY CHERYL L. COX,* BSN, CLASS OF 1970

Curious how life works! Some precipitating event comes out of nowhere, and you are thrust deeply into reflection on those life experiences which for years have been nicely tucked away. It is not that those experiences are unpleasant to recall; it is more that certain life events actually define you, and you live them rather than remember their origins. So, when Dianne Greenhill called me a week before my 49th birthday; her request — "Would/could you write something about what, if anything, the College of Nursing contributed to your career?" For my colleague and long-time friend, the would was an unconditional yes; the could has proven to be an enormous challenge which may require a lifetime to complete? How does one adequately describe an institution and the people within it that by design carefully crafted and molded not only the professional, but to a large extent the person that I strive to become? I offer the following as a reflection and what, I hope, is a tribute to those who gave their very best so that I might in turn do the same for patients, the profession, and important people in my life.

The skills and characteristics which were "gifted" to me at UTCN started arriving long before my admission. For an unknown 16-year-old high school junior living in Fort Wayne, Indiana and planning a pre-nursing curriculum, Grace Wallace translated the then terrible foreign and confusing MSU undergraduate catalog into a four-semester curricular plan which served as a template to begin my nursing education. She began to lay the base that would prove to be so critical to my development as a professional nurse and a confident human being. From Grace Wallace, I learned that everyone is important and deserves the best you have to offer at each encounter. No request is too trivial and attention to detail is a virtue! As I made the transition from pre-nursing to nursing, Grace Wallace once again was there with important life lessons; I wanted to come

to UT after only one year of pre-nursing; Grace, with firm tenderness strongly urged me to complete a second year at MSU, but I could not wait to "be a nurse." Reluctantly, she supported my admission, while providing sufficient data to allow me to make an informed choice. Gracie, you were right; I struggled to blend the science and humanities in those first and second years at UT! Life is filled with choice, but they should always be informed choices with exquisite detail about their consequences! Self-determinism, motivation and perceived competency energize the theoretical model which has guided my nursing research career!

Lessons in strength, values, courage, love, tenderness, grief, conflict, accuracy, detail and commitment constituted the bulk of the curriculum for the next two years. Some of those lessons were harder to learn than others; some

Pictured left to right are Cheryl Cox, Ruth Neil Murry, Mary Anne Grim, Sandra Peal, and Carol Ann Thompson viewing model of new Student Alumni Center in July 1969.

of those lessons were exhilarating; and some of those lessons were only fully realized years after the fact. The really important and sustaining lessons for me as nurse and person came not as blaring classroom content, but were conveyed out of the very fabric of the humanity reflected in those who taught me. To watch Dr. Allen Battle, through compassion and gentle, but highly calculated skill, extract critical information from frightened and confused patients originating from worlds so different from his own, taught me the notion of professional adaptation; that premise is now reflected prominently in my own theoretical and research efforts about client singularity and client/professional interaction.

Being with Elinor Reed at the bedside of a dying patient, taught me gentleness of voice, tenderness of touch, and the ability to convey love and meaningfulness at the time it was most

needed. Those actions are reflected, I hope, in the concept/construct of affective support and response in my evolving conceptual framework. Elinor showed me that while perfection may not always be attained, it must always be the goal; to try for less is to be less than what our potential may dictate.

From Dorothy Hocker, I learned that the patient is a complex, integrated whole; the nurse is strictly accountable for every detail that may contribute to that patient's well-being and/or result in harm. Accuracy, detail and repeated validation, together with a constant working knowledge of the basic sciences, were to be everyday tools in the clinical arena. Inaccurate or outdated knowledge was an abomination! Those lessons are reflected in my current work on the concept of professional/technical competencies as an important explanatory variable in patient health outcomes.

Our rudimentary skills launched, we were now ready to face greater life complexities in our final year at UTCN. Mildred Proctor, Jane Brennan and Dianne Greenhill taught us the reality then, of what is now politically chic — diversity, multiculturalism, the physically, mentally, and socially challenged, managed care without resources. For me, the most important lesson was that, unequivocally, the nurse can make a difference — immediate, short-term and far reaching differences. I wanted to address those differences; I learned to address the immediate and short-term difference by becoming a family nurse practitioner; I would like to think that I am learning to address the long-term differences though my research efforts on health behavior and professional intervention.

While all these life lessons were being absorbed, there was an ever-pervasive presence of one who reflected beautifully all that I wanted to become as a nurse and person. Ruth Neil Murry was the closest to royalty that I have ever been. Perhaps her crown, scepter, and robes were of my own design, but they were there and they rightfully belonged to her. She had the ability to silence a room with her presence; with sharp wit and preconceived strategies she effected her agendas; she commanded respect in academic and non-academic circles alike, and she pursued her life in a manner consistent with her values and life goals independent of contemporary social sanctions. She was a teacher, mentor and life role model for me. From her I learned courage and persistence; I

learned about commitment to cause and commitment to friends and colleagues. I learned gentleness of presentation undergirded by strength of conviction. I strive daily to become what she believed I could be, and to reflect in me what I so admired in her. I know that she is now in a place where she can be watchful and guiding over so many of us as we continue our efforts in this life.

Obviously UTCN's significance to me is not easily captured in a few words. It provided the philosophical base for my view on nursing practice; it gave me, through classroom, clinical, and faculty modeling, the critical content for explicating what nursing is and what nursing does to effect positive health outcomes for all patients independent of setting, health status or social and environmental circumstances. Its five-year curriculum provided a strong liberal arts exposure and a strong basic and social science and clinical experience base. This curriculum and those who implemented it prepared me for a life of learning, inquiry and pleasure that would not have been within my reach with a narrower and less intensive curriculum. The faculty and Dean modeled professional nursing, and they modeled life; for me, these were powerful and positive forces in charting my own professional and life course. As we celebrate our 100th year as an institution of professional nursing. I want to thank THE COLLEGE for its contribution to who and what I am today. I sincerely, hope that my professional contributions accurately reflect the bounty I was given.

*Cheryl L. Cox, *after graduation from UT in 1970, earned her MSN at Vanderbilt University in 1972 and her PhD from the University of Rochester, New York in 1982. She has practiced as a Family Nurse Clinician.* ✦ *Her past faculty positions have been at the University of Tennessee, Memphis and University of Illinois at Chicago where she was a tenured Associate Professor and Research Director. Currently she is a Professor of Nursing at the University of Massachusetts, Lowell, where she is engaged in research and directs the doctoral program.* ✦

CHAPTER SIX

Movement Toward Graduate Education

1971-1990s

A Tennessee study of "The Need, Supply, and Education of Professional Nurses" was requested by the legislature and completed in 1968. A nurse crisis was identified and recommendations were made that the state expand nursing education programs. The University of Tennessee was recommended to establish or expand nursing programs including a master's degree at UT Memphis. The Tennessee Higher Education Commission formed a Board of Consultants for Nursing Education in Tennessee consisting of seven distinguished educators. Ms. Inez Haynes of the National League for Nursing and Ms. Jessie Scott of the US Public Health Service were included in the group.

Dr. Shirley Burd
Professor and Graduate
Director
Community-Mental
Health Nursing

This Board's report of July 1969 also mentioned "shortages of properly qualified nursing personnel in Tennessee are serious and statewide," and that "costs of nursing education was high partly due to small enrollments." Recommendations included exploring ways to assist faculty in obtaining the master's degree in nursing. One of these was to establish a master's degree program at UT Memphis. Other recommendations were to establish new bachelor's degree programs at UT Chattanooga (1970), UT Knoxville (1970) and at Memphis State University. The program at UT Memphis was recommended to double in size. "At some future time a doctor's degree program in a public institution in the state" should be established. The consultants also "noticed that the number of black students in nursing education is small… and it believes that schools should make special efforts to recruit qualified black students into nursing." (Survey of Nursing Education in Tennessee, 1969)

Based on the survey recommending that a graduate program in nursing be established at UT Memphis, the faculty proposed a program for approval. On February 3, 1969, the Board

of Trustees approved the proposal and sent a recommendation to the Tennessee Higher Education Commission. Funding was requested for both 1969-70 and 1970-71 school years but was not made available. A small appropriation of funds allowed the College to begin planning. The position of Assistant Dean in charge of graduate education was filled in January 1972. A Forum on Graduate Education was held in March to discuss the directions and needs for graduate education in nursing. At the invitation of Dean Murry, 39 Tennessee nurses representing schools of nursing, agencies, professional associations, and regulatory agencies participated. Three doctorally prepared nurse educators were appointed as graduate directors. Dr. Mary Morris was joined by Dr. Beverly Bowns and Dr. Shirley Burd.

In 1972-1973 the program was developed and students were admitted for the 1973 summer quarter. The first students were enrolled in either Community Health Family Nursing preparing family nurse clinicians or Community-Mental Health Nursing. All graduate students had a functional area in teaching as required by the Tennessee Higher Education

Commission. During the following year, Physical Illness Nursing was added. Originally, the program offered the MS degree with a major in nursing and was under the graduate school. It was a five-quarter program including a core of medical science, education, systems, and research courses. A professional paper rather than a thesis was completed for the research requirement. Credits required for the degree ranged from 65 to 73 quarter hours depending on the clinical major. A revision in 1977 reduced the total credit hours by making the functional teaching track optional rather than required. Changes were also made in the core courses for all three clinical majors. The governance of the graduate program became entirely a College of Nursing function on January 1, 1980, and the degree granted became the Master of Science in Nursing. Around this same time, Physical Illness Nursing became Medical and Surgical Nursing. A concentration in Maternal and Child Nursing was added in 1984; Nursing Administration and Public Health/Community Health Nursing in 1986. The anesthesia certificate program located at the UT Medical Center at Knoxville became a master's option in 1993.

Two major continuing education projects of the College were the pediatric associate program and the adult nurse practitioner program. The pediatric associate program was initiated in the Spring of 1972 for a few selected students as an extension of the undergraduate curriculum. The adult nurse practitioner program was initiated in the Spring of 1973. The adult program was conducted jointly by the College of Nursing and Medicine and consisted of a 28 week didactic and 12 week preceptorship leading to a certificate.

An accelerated baccalaureate program in nursing for individuals holding a baccalaureate degree in another field was funded by the Department of Health, Education, and Welfare for three years. Two classes graduated by September 1976. The program was discontinued when grant money was no longer available. An accelerated option of the baccalaureate curriculum was again instituted in May 1989 for those individuals with a baccalaureate in another field, a GPA of at least 3.0 and a GRE score of 1000.

The physical location of the College

(top left) Cheryl Stegbauer teaching nurse practitioner class in 1977
(top right) 1976 Student skit
(bottom) Accelerated program brochure

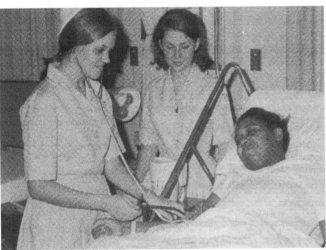

(top left) Students in Goodman House Office, 1979
(top center) Goodman House
(top right) Lamar Alexander Building
(bottom left) Hospital Clinical scene
(bottom right) Undergraduate student officers, 1979

changed in 1973. Lindsley Hall was demolished to permit construction of a combination basic science and education classroom building for the entire campus called the General Education Building (GEB). Nursing was moved to the sixth and seventh floors of the old Goodman House residence. This was to be a "temporary" home until a new combined nursing-library complex was constructed. Nursing actually remained in the Goodman House until 1988 when the College moved to the sixth floor of the Lamar Alexander Building at 877 Madison. In 1985, the Lamar Alexander Building was completed behind the GEB. The Lamar Alexander Building sits on the site of the old Lindsley Hall.

At the time of the 1976 NLN accreditation report, there were "36 academically qualified professional nurses employed as faculty." Seven of these faculty held earned doctorates; plus an additional six were working on or completing doctoral study, demonstrating the continuing improvement in qualifications of the faculty. The NLN awarded the graduate program initial accreditation and the undergraduate program continuing accreditation at the 1976 review.

The length of the baccalaureate program changed in the 70's. For graduates of 1968 through 1976, the program was five years in length with 223 quarter hours required for graduation. As a result of curriculum study in 1970-71, this was reduced to 189 quarter hours with one year of pre-nursing and three years on

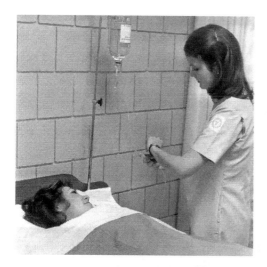

the Memphis campus. Early in 1976, the decision was made to change from a three to a two-year upper division major on the Memphis campus, based on two years of prerequisite work. Most of the basic science courses previously taught on this campus during the nursing major had become available in other colleges from which the applicants to the College had come. Implementation of the two-year upper division major in nursing began in the Fall of 1977. While the specific courses in the curriculum changed, the pattern of the two years upper division major continued into the 1990's. Registered nurses were admitted with advanced standing through various mechanisms such as challenge examination and credit by validation.

The close of 1977 marked the end of an era for the College. Miss Ruth Neil Murry, who had served as Dean since the college had become an autonomous unit in 1949, retired effective December 31, 1977, and was named Emeritus Dean. Miss Murry was active in college alumni activities until prevented by illness. She died on September 7, 1995.

There was a rapid turnover in the leadership of the College of Nursing after Miss Murry's retirement. Dr. Norma Long, who had served as Department Chair and later Associate Dean, became Acting Dean and served from 1978-1979. Dr. Marie Josberger assumed the office in July 1979 and resigned in March 1981. Dr. E. Dianne Greenhill served as Interim Dean, through a difficult period, until November

(top left) Patient care scene, late 1970s-1980s

(top center) Dr. Norma J. Long, Professor and Associate Dean, 1980

(top right) Undergraduate students, 1981

(bottom left) Brenda Smith (right) with nursing visitor from Turkey

(bottom right) 1979 student picnic

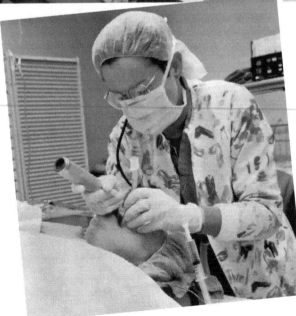

(top left) Undergraduate classroom scene, 1996
(top right) Graduate students participating in Interactive Television
Class transmitted from Memphis to Knoxville. Rachel Taylor, faculty
shown on screen, 1997
(center and bottom) Graduate student and faculty scenes, 1990s

FROM DIPLOMA TO DOCTORATE:

1982. Dr. Michael Allen Carter was appointed Dean effective November 1, 1982, and continues to serve in that role. Dr. Carter came from the University of Colorado where he had served as Chair of the Medical-Surgical Nursing Department. His master's degree is from the University of Arkansas College of Nursing and his DNSc degree in Nursing Science from Boston University School of Nursing. Dr. Carter is a fellow in the American Academy of Nursing; in 1982 he was the youngest to be admitted to fellowship.

As greater emphasis was placed on the graduate program, the size of the undergraduate program was purposefully reduced. The last students to receive the baccalaureate in nursing were admitted July 1996. The UT Board of Trustees acted June 1997 to suspend the undergraduate program effective December of the same year. The last group of undergraduates graduated December 1997, allowing the College to focus entirely on graduate education. West Tennessee had two public and two private educational institutions who were expected to fill the need for undergraduate education. The faculty set as a goal for the College the offering of a professional clinical doctorate to meet the future needs of the increasingly complex health care environment in Tennessee and the nation.

(top) December 1997 undergraduate class preparing for NCLEX (State Board)
(center left) June 1997 grads
(center right) Muriel Rice, Assistant Dean for Students, 1997
(left) Alumna and graduate faculty – Drs. Brenda Mills and Mona Wicks, 1997

Development of the Family Nurse Practitioner Graduate Program

BY BEVERLY BOWNS,* DrPH

I was asked to write about how the Family Nurse Clinician (FNC) graduate program came to be at The University of Tennessee College of Nursing. I guess it could be said simply, that after two years at Vanderbilt, the program moved to UT in 1972. However, if this was all there was to say, it would be presenting a very limited view of what it actually takes to develop a graduate FNC program that was the first of its kind in the nation. The designation of "nurse clinician" was used in those early years to differentiate the master's graduate from the graduate of the certificate programs.

Dr. Beverly Bowns, Professor and Director of Family Nurse Clinician Program, 1972

Private institutions of quality, such as Vanderbilt, maintain the cutting edge of education through experimentation. The program had to be rigorously pre-tested, and Vanderbilt provided this avenue. It was there in 1970, that two courageous students, Kathleen Arganbright and Betsy Hazelwood, agreed to be the "guinea pigs" for 15 months while the curriculum and clinical experiences were identified, developed, and outcomes measured. In 1971 the first class at Vanderbilt was admitted while the trial students were doing their internships.

Cheryl Cox, a BSN graduate from UT Memphis, was a member of that class. The first class graduated in 1972 from the four-term, 12-month program. It was time to move the program to a public institution where we could tap a larger pool of prospective students.

Ruth Neil Murry was aware of this need and recruited me to UT Memphis to develop the FNC program. After obtaining a generous federal grant, we began to prepare for the program in its new location. This does not mean to imply that such a controversial program and one that would take longer than any other graduate program to complete, would be readily accepted. It was not for lack of students; they came from every corner of the United States. On the other hand, the medical school faculty needed to be involved in the early stage. This required some persuasion and acceptance in order to have the physicians' time commitment since they would be the initial instructors for the FNC program. I then recruited two master's prepared FNC faculty who were graduates of the new program at Texas Woman's University, Houston. I served as a consultant to the Texas program, and Karen Radke and Cheryl Cummings (Stegbauer) were brought to UT Memphis to serve as faculty in the College of Nursing. Pat Brisley and Barbara Reid also were early nursing faculty in the FNC program. Patricia Brisley was a nursing faculty member who went through the FNC program with early students and then taught in the FNC program. Barbara Reid was another early faculty member who was important to instruction and grant development activities. Later on, graduates of the program, who were in practice, would become the preceptors and instructors. Yet that is not the full story either. This article, if it does nothing else, will need to help others to see that it takes perseverance and drive that only comes from a strong belief in an idea that just can not be ignored. Although I do not think it needs to be as arduous a route as my own, but it does give an example of the process. The motto perhaps "If they say it can not be done, take it as a sign that it should be done." For me, it was because I had lived through so many experiences, and I had seen so many things being done for all the wrong reasons and in too many wrong ways. Both the consumer of health care and the nurse as a provider were being short changed.

I graduated from the 12th grade in 1944 and announced to my parents I wanted to be a nurse. Stunned, they made it clear they had no intention of paying for my college education for me to become a nurse. The compromise was to have me enroll in a hospital program where I would be enlightened. They knew I would be home in one year, ready to join my brother at Stanford. They gave me a round trip ticket to San Francisco where I completed three years of training and was "ready" to start my career as a Public Health Nurse.

Although I had selected a school that was affiliated with the Berkeley Medical School, it still was just a vocational education. At the time, I had refused to acknowledge that fact. Early in my practice as a Public Health Nurse, I realized my knowledge and my technical skills were lacking. At best, I was prepared to be a hospital nurse and hand maiden to physicians. But I did not practice in a hospital, nor did the other P.H. nurses working with me. I hit the medical books at night, visited the university library, and picked the brains of physicians, pharmacists, commissioners, and public health officials in order to do what needed to be done. I discovered that much of a family's health care was left up to chance, and very little was maintaining wellness; yet, there was so much evidence that it could be different. Public Health Nurses (PHN) are given

tremendous responsibility with the authority always being in the hand of "others."

In "my day" responsibilities of the PHN included deliveries in the home; follow-up on tuberculosis and sexually transmitted diseases; two polio epidemics; childhood communicable diseases and quarantine procedures; child health and crippled children clinics in small communities throughout the county; and Indian Services that meant covering care of the Shoshone and Bannock Indians on the Fort Hall Reservation in Idaho. Every experience opened new vistas and required new strategies for applying my skills. I kept copious annotative records of events and experiences. After marriage and two short stints at the University of Washington and the University of Minnesota, I knew things could and should be different. I had to go back to school.

My formal education began when I attended Columbia University to obtain a BSN. It was a small step in the right direction. After completing two majors at the University of Minnesota in Public Health Mental Health and Education and two majors at Johns Hopkins in Family Therapy and Administration, I had what I believed was needed.

Obstacles were expected, but what was not expected was to discover mainstream nursing was promoting what was called the Nurse Practitioner Program (NP). They were "popping up" all over the country. These programs would force some nurses into a career life that I had managed, at great cost, to put behind me. Some of these programs would be anywhere from six weeks to six months, and that was merely "patch-work learning." Physician's Assistant Programs also were being developed and became confused with programs like ours. It was important to have the nursing division of the U.S. Public Health Service be aware of the ramifications of the direction nursing seemed to be bent on pursuing.

At this time, Fay Abdullah was providing the leadership in P.H. Nursing in the National

Public Health Service. I pleaded for these "new" skills of physical examination to be introduced in the BSN programs and for them including a higher level and standard of physical examination skills for the MSN clinician in Public Health. I pointed out that, after all, this is where the greater part of nursing was eventually going to be conducted. I explained that "Practitioner" was a catch word since all nurses, at all levels and in any service are practitioners. I became aware it was political and related to a language that would enable schools of nursing to obtain grants and get funding. This time I did not win. Nevertheless the FNC program survived and thrived.

Philosophy is critical as it gives direction to any program. This I believed: 1) the program would be family centered to keep costs down, to be comprehensive, and provide for quality of care, and a support group in health and illness should be considered essential; 2) the program must be community based because that is where the largest percent of the action is needed. After all, only a small percent of the population ever required hospitalization; 3) prevention and all other Public Health Principles basic to health care practice would be incorporated in the curriculum; 4) wellness was key to establish a mindset conducive to accepting all health care actions that focus practice on strengths of a family or any one member who is receiving care, and emphasis was on an economy of good health care and quality of life; and 5) all clinical faculty were to be in active practice, and all faculty teaching theory would return to practice on a regular basis, i.e. every other summer or several times a week; this was essential to keep reality a part of theory development.

Graduate student examining patient

These philosophical tenets were accepted by Dean Murry and adhered to by the graduate faculty and the students. The sciences in the curriculum were advanced Physiology, Pharmacology and Pathology, Epidemiology and Research. Technology included Physical Examination Process, Family Systems Analysis, Group Dynamics in Interviewing and Therapeutic Communications. The technical skills required in conducting a physical examination and use of the tools as extensors caused a "Red Flag," and caused a negative reaction among some of the other health professionals. The liberal use of instruments such as stethoscope, otoscope, ophthalmoscope and a pen light by nurses was unfamiliar and to some inappropriate. Interpretation of lab reports by nurses as they verified and clarified their assessment results had never been done before.

Another red flag was the use of the term "diagnosis" in relation to a nurse's finding. My auto mechanic used a stethoscope and computer, and he handed me an itemized diagnosis (actual heading on the sheet) of his findings and a list of repairs needed in order for my car to run well. A policeman at an accident said to me, "I have to diagnose the circumstances of this situation before I can tell you what I intend to do." Parents treated their family members after they diagnosed a common illness and "prescribed" an over-the-counter medication or folk remedy. These terms were not necessarily conceptually "owned" by but one segment of health care professionals.

"Prescribe" is a third red flag area. Here again is why any nurse, BSN or advanced degree prepared, should know over-the-counter drugs very well. We know every family's medicine cabinet has some over-the-counter medicine and many are contraindicated. Some prescription medications are used liberally and need not be. So it goes. Enough about the traditional barriers to the practice of nursing, after all, that was 25 years ago.

It is not only the variety of experiences, but it is the quality and degree of challenge the experience brings to one's practice that makes for greater expertise. Opening the Rape Crisis Center for FNC students was one example. Concerns that police were insensitive to the victim of sexual assault first alerted me to the problem. Female officers were enlisted to help, but we discovered that this change did not address the issue of sensitive care to victims of rape. We decided no matter what happened to the client before she was discovered and brought under care, it would mean the FNC's therapeutic counseling would be needed at the Rape Crisis Center to help the client through her shock phase of the rape, and for follow up in recovery. I immediately contacted the Forensic Center to understand the scope of care this new experience would demand of the student. Soon we had protocols drawn up to see that the roles of the FNC, police, forensic personnel and the women's clinical staff did not overlap or come into conflict. Also, follow-up would be provided for all clients who desired it. As I understand it, this clinical service provided by nurse practitioners has continued to the present.

Rural experiences were numerous, but urban ones began to open up too. Soon FNC students were in clinics in the low income areas, and home visiting as follow-up on specific physician's referrals began to occur. Later, this referral system became common in large cities over the country. This is called "outreach." As the FNC's gained respect and self-reliance, they were in demand. Professionalism was being realized even with some politically imposed restrictions that would limit the degree of autonomy we sought.

Learning is a life-long experience, and each student became more and more aware of the responsibility she/he was assuming. From time to time, they would ask, "Dr. Bowns, you know there is always so much that is new and yet to be learned, you will need to provide for updating sessions to keep us good." I wonder if that happened at UT after I left? We often discussed in seminar where nursing was going in general and FNC nursing specifically. Breaking mind sets and breaking with the conventional mode was bound to bring FNC's into confrontational interactions. None seemed to believe it would not be something they could not handle, yet they too realized it would be important to have a support system. They often turned to ANA Primary Care section for this. I never knew if they found that met their need.

After 40 years of trying to move nursing in a new direction and not always succeeding, I am happy to leave it to younger people. My only regret is it takes nursing so long to define a clear

*Beverly Henry Bowns *graduated from Franklin Hospital School of Nursing and received her BSN from Teachers College, Columbia.* ✦ *She received her MPH from the University of Minnesota and the DrPH in Mental Health from Johns Hopkins School of Hygiene and Public Health.* ✦ *She taught at the University of California, University of Maryland, and Vanderbilt University prior to coming to UT as Professor and Director of the Community Health Family Nursing Graduate Program from 1972-1977.* ✦ *She served as Dean and Professor of Nursing at Rutger's University. She is currently retired and living in New Jersey.* ✦ *EDITOR'S NOTE: Dr. Bowns passed away in 2004 after the original publication of this history.* ✦

direction and to keep it in focus. Today I am a member of a Board of Education for a region where I have the responsibility to see that public education will gain the attention and support of tax payers at a more basic level. It is another political arena that demands about 30 hours a week of this old retiree's time. I never liked

politics all that much, but if its education, its political. Oh, well!

My best wishes to all of the UT's successes for now and in the future. If anyone is sitting on a dream of an idea, I hope I gave you heart, and you do something about it. It has to "hatch" if you are to realize the greatest of all satisfaction.

Development of the Medical and Surgical Nursing (Physical Nursing) Graduate Program

BY MARY L. SHANNON,* EdD

Dr. Mary L. Morris was appointed Director of the new Physical Illness graduate program in 1972 by Dean Ruth Neil Murry. Dr. Morris worked with Drs. Shirley Burd and Beverly Bowns to plan the initial curriculum that would make up all three majors of the graduate program. The first class of the Physical Illness major entered the program in July 1974. The entering class of around five or six students was predominantly composed of baccalaureate graduates who were on the staff of Baptist Memorial Hospital.

Dr. Mary Lou Shannon
Professor, Medical
Surgical Nursing

EDITOR'S NOTE:
Dr. Morris passed away
in 1997.

For the first few years of the program, students were prepared as generalists in physical illness nursing and were provided with role preparation in education as well. Their clinical practicum experiences were held at Baptist Memorial Hospital. In the first year or two of the program, Dr. Morris was assisted by Kay Nickey, a master's prepared faculty member. Both Dr. Morris and Ms. Nickey provided the bulk of the classes, but they often obtained guest speakers to provide the students with exposure to other medical-surgical faculty members. I taught several classes for her; Elizabeth Stokes and Ruth Smith provided classes as well.

Dr. Morris had wanted me to join the graduate faculty from its inception, but I was busy with the duties of Second Year Chair of the Undergraduate Program, and Dean Murry had asked me to remain in that spot until the graduate physical illness major increased its

enrollment and a suitable chairman could be found for the Second Year Nursing Department. In 1977 I resigned as Second Year Chair and took a position as Professor in the physical illness track.

Both Dr. Morris and I immediately turned our efforts to an analysis of the changes that were taking place with respect to the advanced practice of nursing. We reviewed a number of well-regarded programs in medical-surgical nursing and looked at the trends that were being discussed at professional meetings and in professional journals. Based on our findings, we began to implement curricular changes that would prepare our graduates with specialty preparation rather than the generalist preparation that had been the case. We also instituted preparation for our graduates as clinical nurse specialists. At that time, we proposed two clinical areas of concentration: cardiovascular nursing and oncology nursing. These choices were made based on what we felt to be 1) areas of student interest, 2) areas of medical excellence in the Memphis community, and 3) areas that we either had expertise in or could gain the requisite experience to offer successfully.

Both Dr. Morris and I felt that we were already prepared in oncology nursing, but we needed to obtain additional education in cardiovascular nursing. To that end, I enrolled in the coronary care nursing course that was offered by Mary Ann Northern at Baptist Hospital. This six-week, certificate course formed the basis for the subsequent work that I did in the cardiovascular concentration. Both Mary and I worked to devise the curriculum for both tracks and to obtain the promise of physician availability to teach some of the pathology and therapeutics in each of these areas. The two areas of concentration were advertised locally to prospective students. To our surprise, only one person was interested in oncology nursing; all others were interested in cardiovascular. The end result, of course, was that oncology nursing was never offered as a specialty.

In the Fall of 1982, students were admitted and the cardiovascular theory courses were taught by three Fellows from the Cardiology Department of the College of Medicine who were obtained with the assistance of Dr. Kossman, then chair of the department. Both Dr. Morris and I attended all classes which the Fellows taught and learned along with the students much detail about cardiovascular pathology, indications for diagnostic testing and the limitations of various tests, therapeutic management

(particularly pharmacologic management), how to listen to heart sounds using the Heart Sound Simulator, how to read abnormal EKG's, etc.

Students in the cardiovascular area were initially precepted in the Cardiology Clinic by the Fellows and their colleagues. In this first clinical experience, they practiced their ability to take a pertinent cardiovascular history and to do a cardiovascular physical examination. Following successful completion of that experience, both Dr. Morris and I supervised their clinical nursing practicum experiences at Baptist Memorial Hospital. We also taught the cardiovascular nursing courses that complimented the cardiovascular theory courses.

Dr. Morris and I also taught the educator courses in teaching and curriculum as well as supervised all of the professional papers that were then required of all master's students in the College. The professional papers differed from the thesis in only one respect: the student did not collect data. They formulated the paper as though their research hypothesis was proven true. Over the years, some students did make the decision to collect information. In most instances, it was retrospective chart data. At least one study actually collected prospective data, and that student's findings have been frequently cited in the professional literature on pressure ulcer prevalence in the nursing home setting.

Following Dr. Morris' retirement, I continued to teach the medical surgical area of concentration. Dr. Elizabeth Stokes, Chair of Medical-Surgical Nursing, assisted me from time to time. My work with the graduate program continued until Dr. Stokes' resignation.

Dr. Shannon with an undergraduate student in the '70s

*Mary L. Shannon, *after receiving her BSN from UT in 1959, earned an MA, MEd and EdD from Teachers College, Columbia University.* ✦ *She taught at UT Memphis from 1964-1989. At UT she was a tenured professor and served as Department Chair and Acting Dean. Since 1989 she has been Chairperson of Medical and Surgical Nursing at the University of Texas-Galveston, School of Nursing.* ✦

Alumni Perspective

BY PHYLLIS SKORGA,* BSN, CLASS OF 1971, MS, CLASS OF 1976

I was recruited for the master's program by Dr. Mary Morris as I was walking through the halls of Baptist Memorial Hospital one day. I graduated from the nursing program at UT in 1971 and knew Dr. Morris as a Chairman in the undergraduate school. I decided to look into the master's program and learned that the curriculum was both innovative and exciting. I appreciated the blending of theory and clinical practice with a major in physical illness and a minor in education. Courses covered many areas of interest from physical examination to pharmacology, pathophysiology, nursing theory, and systems development. Clinical practice encompassed several advanced experiences including clinic rounds with cardiology fellows providing care for acute and chronically ill patients with cardiovascular disease. We were also afforded the opportunity to independently set up courses and practice settings in areas of particular interest.

Phyllis Skorga
BSN, Class of 1971
MS, Class of 1976

I remember developing learning experiences in a cardiovascular laboratory to study noninvasive and invasive diagnostic procedures with emphasis on pre and post-procedure patient examinations, analysis of findings, patient/caregiver communications, and education. I also was able to participate in an independent learning experience developed cooperatively with the mental health nursing graduate program.

This course resulted in a political internship in a congressional office in Washington, D.C., to study health care legislation. Based on experiences, I co-authored a document comparing several proposals for national health legislation that the congressmen mailed to health care professionals in the Memphis area to educate and generate feedback. When I reflect back on my experiences in the UT graduate program, I remember countless opportunities!

Dr. Morris was well known in the nursing community as a respected leader. For graduate students, she provided guidance in course work,

assistance in obtaining grants, traineeships, and part-time employment in an effort to facilitate completion of the program of study. She also was available to students to discuss personal issues, problems and needs. I remember a conversation when Dr. Morris reflected on the importance of interpersonal relationships and family for happy living. She was a source of strength and knowledge for all of the students in the class.

The Class of '76 was triple the size of the preceding year's class, and the students were young, bright, eager and motivated to achieve success. Although we were independent, as a class we also studied, worked on projects, and socialized together. We had dreams of ongoing careers in nursing as educators, managers, and clinicians. In particular, the clinical nurse specialist role appeared intriguing, especially the potential for innovative nursing as a change agent.

(left) BSN Class of 1971, Skorga far left, fourth row
(above) Dr. Mary Morris, Emeritus Professor of Nursing, 1995

In our graduate program, Dr. Morris emphasized professionalism and nursing theory, often discussing the points that Margaretta Styles made in her book *Toward a Theory of Nursing*. In the mid 1970's, nurses were struggling to achieve generally accepted theories for the profession. Through our graduate studies, we were challenged to promote growth in the profession by our own example and through ongoing studies. The graduate program was an important life event for all of us with a treasured set of memories and learning experiences that helped to define our careers as graduate nursing professionals.

Phyllis Skorga *graduated from UT Memphis with a BSN in 1971 and MS in 1976. She completed a PhD at the University of Kansas.* ✦ *During her career she has worked clinically in cardiovascular nursing, critical care nursing, and has functioned as a clinical nurse specialist and nursing educator. She currently holds the position of Senior Director of Medical Services at Southern Health Plan, Inc. in Memphis.* ✦

Alumni Perspective

BY MARGARET THORMAN HARTIG,* MS, CLASS OF 1977, PhD, 1993

Then

I first heard of The University of Tennessee, Memphis and the Family Nurse Practitioner program in 1974. I was fortunate to have gone to undergraduate school at the University of Kansas with excellent nurse practitioner role models. When I asked nurse practitioner faculty for recommendations for a master's program, I noticed that UT was always among the top three choices.

Dr. Peg Hartig, Assistant Professor, University of Tennessee Memphis, College of Nursing

I requested information from nurse practitioner programs all over the country, following up on faculty recommendations. Most programs were specialized, and the information I received seemed very restrictive. In contrast, the UT syllabus was broad in scope and had a strong emphasis on family counseling. The minute I read the syllabus, I was convinced the faculty had created the ideal program for me.

I met with Dr. Beverly Bowns, the director of the family nurse practitioner program. I was very impressed with the energy of this slender, dynamic woman. She was very gracious and wanted to know all about me and my goals. She helped confirm that UT was the program for me. After discussion with Bev, as we familiarly referred to her, the Graduate Record Exam and a pile of forms later, I was accepted as a student for the nurse practitioner program. I entered the FNP program in July 1975 as one of two part-time and five full-time students which was a large class at that time. Not many people were crazy enough to try this still new role!

During my first year, I concentrated on completing theory courses. There was still much unknown about the background we would need to implement the nurse practitioner role successfully. It also was anticipated that many of us would be in rural areas with limited resources. Therefore, our course work covered a broad spectrum of knowledge we might possibly need. Course work included not only nursing theory and ethical issues, but also the American education system and teaching/learning theories. We also stumbled through three semesters of statistics and epidemiology, though our instructor, Dr. Joan Zurhelen, made it a lot more manageable than many of us thought possible.

During the second year, I finally spent more time with the clinical faculty, including the very supportive Pat Brisley and Barbara Reid. My first course was physical assessment. I loved that I was finally getting exposed to clinical content. My work responsibilities as a visiting nurse in rural Arkansas gave me plenty of opportunity to implement my new physical assessment skills. I was luckier than many of my classmates to have a ready supply of patients for practice. Many of them quickly went through the patience of their families and neighbors; some even discovering the possibilities of examining family pets! I soon realized how much adding even these skills advanced my practice and my ability to care for patients.

Clinical experiences were intensive and

consumed at least 16 hours per week, not including at least an equal amount of preparation. We were usually paired with a clinical partner who provided both moral support and positive competition. Clinical assignments were divided according to physiologic systems and medical specialties, rather than the integrated, holistic experiences students have today. This division was no doubt influenced in part by the availability of preceptors, who were mainly physicians.

There were not many nurse practitioner role models, and most of our preceptors were physicians. We often had to rely on discussions with faculty and student colleagues to surmise how we would develop the nurse practitioner role. This is not to imply that our physician preceptors were second best, for on the contrary, they were very supportive in guiding our learning. It is also interesting to note that most are now, 20 years later, recognized as being among the best physicians in the city.

Of the many preceptors who are remembered, many memories of personality as well as clinical learning are associated with Dr. Lillian "Diamond Lil" Cox. Her clinical intuition and diagnostic skills were even more impressive than the rings on her fingers that earned her the affectionate nickname. Our experience with her was intended to focus on cardiovascular issues. In reality, she taught us much about considering the whole patient and looking beyond one's specialty area.

We were often treated as medical students and given the same challenges and opportunities. Unfortunately our welcome was more often marred by staff nurses once they realized we were not medical students. They were not quite sure what to do with us, since we were not trying to deny being nurses. Some nurses accused us of thinking we were smarter or better than they. Fortunately, a little persistence and reassurance won over most nurses whom we encountered.

Clinical experiences occurred at the Veteran's Administration Hospital, UT clinics, and community clinics. My cardiovascular, neurology, and adult/ambulatory experiences were at the VA. Respiratory care was addressed at the old Chest Hospital. Obstetric and gynecology experiences were at Gailor Clinic. Several classmates also met their requirement of delivering at least one baby by spending hours awaiting their opportunity at the now demolished John Gaston Hospital. Pediatric experiences usually took place in community clinics. For many of us, our only nurse practitioner contacts came in these clinics. Even then, there were some differences because many of the nurse practitioners in Memphis at that time were graduates of a popular certificate program conducted by UT. This program was eventually phased out, and the master's level program survived. It is important to note that despite the differences in education, many of these early nurse practitioners brought a wide breadth of experience and ability to the role that was invaluable to our learning.

Clinical conferences were the intensive theory component of the clinical courses. Students participated actively with alternating responsibility for presenting content. Since there were not many students, we had plenty of "opportunities" for presentation. Student presentations were interspersed with faculty and guest lectures. We also dealt with other topics, such as legal and political issues. The family counseling course provided another clinical experience. We would meet our assigned family at their home and audiotape our interactions. We would then meet as a group, review the tapes and our written logs, and receive feedback and recommendations from the group. While this course could not compete with the intensive and extensive experiences in which the psychiatric family nurse practitioner students are now involved, the knowledge I gained in the course has always given me important insights

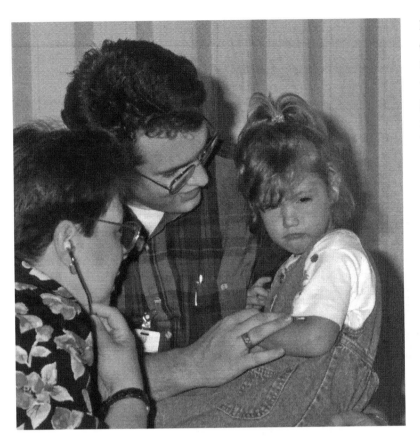

Hartig examining child

in personal and clinical situations.

Lest current students think we avoided the sometimes dreaded thesis requirement, we did complete a professional paper. The professional paper required a clinical research question, review of literature, and discussion of the question. Unlike the thesis, we did not actually conduct the research. Rather, we put those additional hours of statistics to work in making an educated guess as to what the results might have been and based our discussion on those suppositions. While that process may seem easier than the thesis, we did not have the same intensity of faculty guidance and support experienced by students now in the program. Those of us who went on to doctoral study also lacked necessary research experience.

The final clinical experience was a 10-week, full-time residency. Like many of my colleagues, I had a rural experience. Mine was at Decatur County Clinic in Parsons, Tennessee.

Parsons is a small town on the Tennessee River east of Jackson. I lived in the hospital next to the clinic during the week and went home on weekends. The hospital provided an empty patient room for me with a private bath. I ate in the hospital kitchen with many of the staff. I only had to walk across the emergency room driveway to the clinic. In addition to the clinic patients, we also visited surrounding rural clinics on occasion. Living in the hospital made it easier when I spent the night awake on call with my physician preceptor. It was during this time that I finally met (and exceeded) my baby delivery requirement. I also felt quite proud of myself by the end of the experience when I was able to see clinic patients while the physician handled emergencies in the hospital.

At last I finished all my course requirements in early September 1977. My final day at UT as a nurse practitioner student included handing in my professional paper and passing an oral examination covering clinical issues. Orals were definitely more anxiety provoking for me than a written examination, but fortunately I survived both. Graduation in December 1977 gave me one last chance to see the class and faculty all together, but fortunately school experiences are remembered fondly whenever I do meet up with former classmates or faculty.

Now

This response to Dr. Greenhill's request to share graduate school experiences brought back many memories I thought were long forgotten. I also became aware of lessons that are with me every day. I always remembered the importance of clinical involvement. This has sometimes been a challenge to me because much of my career has been in academia. My respect for the faculty members' passion for clinical involvement and its importance to advancing the nursing profession and my own personal fulfillment has kept me active in clinical care. I have even had some fun with the challenge of developing new clinical sites when established sites were not available.

I have learned it is acceptable to not know everything. Actually it is unrealistic because of the broad nature of the role. Rather, it is important to be aware of and honest about what you do and do not know. I have still vivid memories of being on rounds with a well-respected cardiologist and a large group of medical students. The cardiologist chose me as the first of the entire group to auscultate an interesting murmur found in a young man with a thin chest. The murmur should have been easy to find. I tried hard to hear what he described, but I just could not. I was well aware that I was the only nurse practitioner student and wanted to vanish as I reported to him what I took to be my failure. He listened on his own to guide me and was very pleased to report that at that time he could not hear the murmur either!

Acceptance of not being omnipotent also carries a companion responsibility to keep learning. The willingness to learn has had the very positive effect of learning a great deal from both nurse practitioner and physician colleagues. Pleasantly, they have been gracious enough to acknowledge they have also learned from me. Lifetime learning led me to my most recent challenge of doctoral education – another fulfilling experience.

I have made an active effort to remember my own anxieties and the processes of role development so as to reassure students that they can get from there to here. I am also firmly committed to the concept of mentoring each other. One of my great excitements has been to consult with and refer to other nurse practitioners. It is a real affirmation of what we have to offer.

I also came away with an unexpected acquisition, my husband and fellow nurse practitioner student, Richard. That baby delivering experience held him in good stead as he has delivered both of our daughters! Our professional experiences are also reflective of the varied pathways our classmates have taken. Several, including Richard, are strongly focused on clinical care. A few, like me, have taken a more academic route. Overlaps do exist. I am actively involved in the College of Nursing's faculty practice activities, and Richard is a regular presence as a guest lecturer and clinical preceptor in his role of volunteer faculty member. He is also my first choice for a reliable and knowledgeable clinical resource.

I have never regretted taking on the challenge of becoming a nurse practitioner. My preparation at UT has always served me well. This role has allowed me a great diversity of experiences, both clinical and academic. As the College of Nursing celebrates 100 years of nursing education, it gives me the opportunity to reflect on the opportunities afforded me by my association with such dedicated faculty. It also gives me new impetus to continue that tradition of contributing to and developing advanced nursing practice in Memphis and beyond.

Margaret (Peg) T. Hartig received her BSN at the University of Kansas and her MSN from UT in 1977. ✦ After completing doctoral courses at the University of Alabama she transferred to UT Memphis where she completed the PhD in 1993. She has been a faculty member at UT Memphis since 1987 where she teaches graduate students and practices as a family nurse practitioner. ✦

Alumni Perspective

BY JUDY CARBAGE MARTIN,* MSN, CLASS OF 1988, PhD, 1996

During the first few years of my nursing career, it was my belief that the epitome of professional nursing was the registered nurse who provides the care of patients during hospitalization. After all, during the late 1970s and early 1980s, the hospital was the site of the majority of diagnostic testing and therapeutic care. Furthermore, admissions for practically any reasons were adequate length to allow substantial sessions of patient and family education to ensure the discharge and transition home would be smooth.

Dr. Judy Martin
Assistant Professor
University of Tennessee
Memphis
College of Nursing

Then came the advent of Diagnosis Related Groups (DRGs). DRGs were introduced by Medicare in approximately 1983 as the basis for prospective pricing of hospital care costs based on the medical diagnoses documented. As you may recall, DRGs caused major disruptions in hospital practices related to length of stay and costing of services. My feelings of satisfaction lessened at patient discharge as I became increasingly aware that my patients were going home earlier, sicker, and with less preparation for what would be required to complete recovery at home. Moreover, I had begun to understand more clearly the importance of health care in the community. I had been disillusioned by the major focus of my diploma education in nursing.

The realization that hospitals could be no longer viewed as the primary site of health care marked a major turning point in my professional development. I found myself increasingly concerned over the apparent diminishing health status of patients at discharge. I was often tormented over the potentially negative outcomes of patients who seemed inadequately recovered and prepared for home care at discharge. My concern regarding patient functioning in the community and their outcomes after discharge prompted my increased interest in community/public health nursing as a specialty.

After graduating with a baccalaureate nursing completion program at Memphis State University, I became a nursing instructor at the Methodist Hospital School of Nursing. During this time, I began attempts to influence the way upcoming nurses would view and care for patients who were hospitalized. The emphasis of my instruction became that of helping patients to return to an optimal level of health and functioning for the rest of their lives. Rather than focusing solely on acute care activities, I attempted to help students see that patients "live in the community," and that our focus must be to influence the way they live after discharge.

This developing philosophy prompted me to research nearby graduate programs offering a community health track and found none that interested me. Reluctantly, I applied to the College of Nursing at UT Memphis, even though I knew that primary care was the only program of community health education available. As fate would have it, I was unable to accept fall placement in the family nurse practitioner (FNP) track as offered by Dr. Chris Garrett. Because of fragile emotions related to recently completing a difficult pregnancy, anticipated guilt over beginning graduate studies with a premature infant, and uncertainty over pursuing a graduate focus that did not exactly fit with my current interest in

FROM DIPLOMA TO DOCTORATE:

care of community groups, I declined admission to the primary care program.

During the next few months I met Dr. Dianne Greenhill. As time went on, she and I conversed about my future career plans related to nursing. Dr. Greenhill described to me her funding proposal for an upcoming Public Health Nursing (PHN) curriculum that would be added to the department of Community Health Family Nursing. This program attracted my interests related to care of patients "where they live." I reactivated my revised application for admission to UT. Finally, I had identified a program I felt would enhance my ability to meet the needs of patients in the community. In the following discussion, I will share my student perspectives of the program, relationships among classmates, and products of the PHN program. Finally, I will share perspectives related to my current status as a nurse educator, practitioner, and researcher.

I can recall the first days of class for our tiny group of six students: Pam Ark, Susie Erstine, Rexann Pickering, Terry Zucconi, Ken Allen, and myself. Following course orientation by Dr. Greenhill, Drs. Leon McAulay and Suzanne Thomas facilitated our completion of the first segment of the program which focused on assessment and care of families. We sat nervously facing each other in one of the small GEB classrooms with wide eyes and hopeful hearts. We all agreed that assignments and class discussions brought to light a number of issues about families that we had not previously understood or considered to be important. It was apparent by the end of the term that our understanding of families had greatly developed.

Another major course in the PHN track was facilitated by Dr. Suzanne Thomas. She helped to develop our understanding of how to systematically assess larger groups of community living individuals. Through the pain staking process of aggregate assessment, we learned how to perform and explore existing characteristics of a group to identify common problems and needs;

the diagnoses (problems and needs) would serve as the basis of intervention program development. At this point Dr. Joy Wachs facilitated our understanding of the step-by-step process of developing health promotion programs in response to those identified aggregate problems. Moreover, we were introduced to mechanisms for demonstrating the potential benefits of a proposed program based on aggregate diagnosis data and cost-benefit or cost-effectiveness analyses, as appropriate. Finally, Drs. Greenhill and Wachs facilitated our learning of how to evaluate properly and effectively a health promotion program.

The PHN track included courses in epidemiology, program planning and evaluation, community diagnosis, and the core courses of nursing theory and research. By far, the two most significant theoretical frameworks I came to appreciate and understand were the Health Belief and the Health Promotion Models. The PHN program certainly served to elucidate for me the critical importance of identifying and enhancing motivators and removing perceived barriers to health promotion and disease prevention.

Dr. Greenhill provided guidance related to the final (5-week) practicum sites and projects based on individual goals following graduation. She also provided assistance in resume' and vita preparation as we pioneered into unexplored territory as the first few public health specialists in this region. This was a time of transition as we neared completion of our programs. I fondly recall that one of the most difficult transitions for me during this time was to begin addressing Dr. Greenhill by her first name, Dianne. Somehow, it just did not seem respectful until after graduation; yet, she insisted, and we complied.

My cohorts of PHN students consisted of adults ranging in age from approximately 28 years to the early 40s. The fact that we had such different previous career backgrounds and future plans related to intended use of that degree we pursued was probably the most peculiar char-

Dr. Christine Garrett with recruitment display

acteristic of our group. Nevertheless, we all felt that the program would meet our personal and professional needs. Bonds formed among cohorts appeared to be directly related to employment and minority status. Neither Pam nor Susie were employed during the program; I can recall wishing that I, too, had been able to afford school without working. Terry commuted home on weekends to northwest Tennessee, but lived in the dormitory during the week so she could devote full attention to her studies. While Ken maintained part-time employment, both Rexann and I continued to work full-time. The most enduring bonds were formed between Pam, Susie, and Terry, as they often spent time together studying or preparing for class. Rexann and I formed a bond that was probably of more benefit to myself than the reverse. She had previously earned a master's degree in education and completed course work toward a doctorate in education; thus graduate education was not a new experience for her. She assisted me in juggling the responsibilities of work to allow ample time for assignment and class preparation. Ken and I shared a warm and special bond in that we were both loners and in that we teased each other about being the minority representation of the class: the one white male and the one black female. We always joked that we would have to be certain to submit quality products because it would be more noticeable if either of us flunked out of the program. Finally, the entire group shared a thread of respect for each other as individuals and support for the efforts and accomplishments of all. We all rejoiced as we

simultaneously progressed through the entire didactic and clinical components of the program.

Graduation occurred at different points for my fellow cohorts from the first PHN program related to varying dates of thesis completion. Terry, Susie, and Rexann were the first graduates completing in December of 1987. Pam and I graduated in June of 1988. Graduation for Ken took place in December of 1989.

Terry resumed employment at a county health department with the intent to promote upward within the organization to an administrative position. Susie was employed by FedEx to provide employee counseling and education on health promotion and disease prevention. Rexann was promoted to coordinator of continuing education for nurses at the Methodist Hospital Systems. Pam was hired as the director of nursing for the Upjohn Home Health (later Trinity). She served in that position for several years until she decided, in later years, to join the faculty at UT Memphis in teaching undergraduate community health nursing.

After graduation, I was offered a faculty position at the College of Nursing at UT Memphis. After one term of orientation with Brenda Mills, I coordinated the theory component of undergraduate nursing for the next three years. Additionally, I precepted students in the clinical component of community health nursing. I was fulfilling my personal goal of providing care and teaching students how to provide care for patients in the community. This responsibility required that I call upon all that I had learned in the PHN program to prepare UT Memphis nursing students for their responsibility to the community's health.

Ken is now deceased as he was stricken with cancer during the last year of his program. Despite his illness, he persevered to successfully complete his master's thesis and graduate before he died. He spent the remaining months that he was employed supervising and providing home health care nursing. I will always remember him and admire his strength.

In my attempt to grow up, I was moved to return to the student role on two later occasions: to pursue preparation for FNP certification and to earn the Doctor of Philosophy degree. As time and opportunity became available, I was encouraged by Dr. Brenda Mills and Dr. Carol Panicucci to proceed with completion of additional courses and clinical as required for certification as a family nurse practitioner. I was convinced that certification as a family nurse practitioner added to the foundational preparation as a public health specialist and broadened my ability to provide students with a rich knowledge and experience of community health in clinic and home settings.

I was reminded annually during evaluation by Dr. Panicucci that I had identified as a major professional goal to earn the doctorate in nursing. Therefore, as a final educational experience I dove into a painful, yet enriching and life-changing experience: doctoral studies. Amazingly, one of the most challenging and stimulating courses included in the curriculum was Philosophy of Science, facilitated by Dr. Michael Carter. Although I was able to master the Biostatistics course offered by Dr. Betsy Tolley, she can attest to the fact that I shed tears in trying to make the numbers mean something for my patients in the community. Completion of these most challenging courses motivated me to complete the doctoral program. Under the mentorship of seasoned researchers and practitioners such as Dr. Veronica Engle, Dr. Marhall Graney, Dr. Marie Gates, Dr. Nan Lackey, Dr. Carol Panicucci and Dr. Michael Carter, I learned to demonstrate, rather than merely teach, the connection between nursing practice, education, and research. As a result, I can help students to comprehend how advanced practice nurses can enhance the functional health and quality of life for various community aggregates. Psycho-emotional support from my husband and children, Momma, church family, and many other friends and colleagues including Ms. Muriel Rice, Dr. Mona Wicks, Ms. Cheryl Johnson, Ms. Anita Boykins, Dr. Dianne Greenhill, Ms. Kathy Stewart, and Ms. Pat Goedecke helped me to persevere.

Not until the graduation date approached, did I realize that I would set a record of firsts in African-American history. Upon graduation in December of 1994, I became the first African-American to earn the PhD in nursing from a Tennessee university. It is surprising that by 1994, this was a first. I believe that it is important that no one should misconstrue this information to think that no previous southern African-Americans have been intelligent or capable of such attainment in the state of Tennessee. A more likely explanation is simply this: There has probably been no African-American who previously had the financial, institutional, spiritual, and familial support to attain this achievement. For these supports, I am forever grateful. As a result of my attainment, I am indebted to offer support, guidance, and mentoring to young African-Americans and others who can benefit from my input in making decisions related to nursing education. I am also indebted to those older adults who have paved the way for me to advance; to them I devote the major focus of my health promotion research.

*Judy Carbage Martin *received her BSN from Memphis State University and completed her MSN at UT Memphis in 1988. ✦ She taught at Methodist School of Nursing in Memphis. She has served as a faculty member at UT Memphis since 1988 and earned her PhD from UT in 1994. Her practice and research are related to older adults. ✦*

Practice Mission of the College

BY MICHAEL A. CARTER,* PROFESSOR AND DEAN

From the early beginning of modern nursing, there was the idea that students would learn from faculty who were providing patient care. The first women who served as the faculty of the program that would become the College of Nursing were also the clinical nursing staff for the Memphis General Hospital. In these early years, it was expected that students would learn from the staff nurse. Many changes were necessary as the program matured and came under the full control of the University, but the strong importance of practice has remained.

UT William F. Bowld Hospital

Several key activities mark the development of the faculty practice. The creation of the William F. Bowld Hospital brought with it the need for the nursing faculty to be involved in the newly created, federally funded Clinical Research Center. A number of projects took place between the College of Nursing and the Memphis and Shelby County Health Department as well as the John Gaston Hospital. Most of these projects, however, were not an integral part of the faculty role. The faculty

had worked hard to build the academic quality of the nursing program and had been clear in distinguishing the BSN from the predominant hospital-based programs in which the students and faculty often were used as staff and often at lower pay.

In the early 1980s, many of the College of Nursing faculty were involved with practice but usually outside of their teaching responsibilities. Faculty worked in the summer or in their time off as clinicians for a variety of organizations. Two exceptions to this were the faculty participation in the operation of the Shrine School and the Head Start physical examinations.

The Shrine School is a large public school in the Memphis Public School system. The students who attend the Shrine School have a number of health conditions that are often disabling. These include conditions such as cerebral palsy and meningomyelocele. The Shrine School contracted with the College of Nursing for the faculty and students to provide direct care services while the students learned. For a number of years, faculty organized and delivered the services, and many students received clinical education at the Shrine School.

The Head Start Program of Memphis provides a number of services to poor, inner-

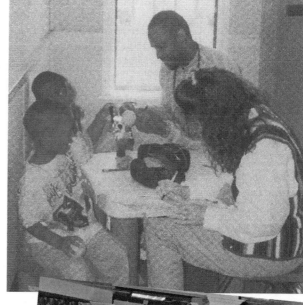

city children. A part of their federal requirement is that the children have yearly physical and developmental examinations. The faculty negotiated a contract with Head Start and Medicaid of Tennessee to provide physical examinations to numerous children in the inner city. Students under faculty supervision provide hundreds of examinations to children in the Head Start Centers each year. Many of these children have little other access to health care. The College was one of the first nursing organizations in the State of Tennessee to apply for and receive its own Medicaid billing number. Medicaid paid the College directly for these services and any children not covered by Medicaid were paid by Head Start. This activity was one of our first community based nursing centers.

From these two early successful faculty practice programs, the faculty developed a number of other services. In the early 1980's, the Student Health Service had a number of problems with availability and quality. Students were displeased with the manner in which they were required to receive health care. The College of Nursing was approved by the Chancellor to begin operation of the service and to make a

number of changes in its operations. The first change was that primary care would be provided by faculty nurse practitioners. The second change was the service was renamed The University Health Service, and was opened to students' families, faculty, staff, and the community. All age groups were included in this model, and for the first time a quality assurance program was put into place. Today, faculty and staff from the College of Nursing operate this service, and the Associate Dean for Academic Affairs, Dr. Peggy Veeser, is the Director.

Also, in the early 1980's, B'Nai B'Rith Hospital and Home for the Aged approached the College about providing nurse practitioner services there. Faculty from the College, including Dr. Cheryl Stegbauer and Dr. Peg Hartig, created an innovative practice at this nursing home. Students in the BSN and MSN program

(left) University Health Service Personnel
(right) UT Nursing Students participating in Head Start Physical Examinations, 1997
(bottom) Drs. Carter and Hartig at the Memphis Jewish Home

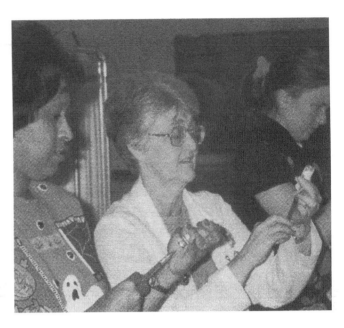

(top left) Faculty and students at Mid-South Family Health Care

(top right) Faculty member Anita Boykins, Kellogg Post-Doctoral Fellow, Dr. Mary Hazzard, and Undergraduate Student Body President Allison Wright preparing flu shots for campus "Boo Flu" Day, October 1996

(center) Dr. Sheldon Korones and Jean Lancaster

(bottom) Fay Russell, '62, Bowling Center for Developmental Disabilities

(right) Dr. Michael Carter with patient at Memphis Jewish Home

received portions of their clinical education there under the direction of the faculty. PhD students conducted research at the nursing home under the direction of the faculty.

From these early beginnings, the faculty have developed a nationally recognized program of practice to support our teaching and research missions. The National Organization of Nurse Practitioner Faculties awarded the College of Nursing their Outstanding Faculty Practice Award in 1995. The selection is made from all nursing faculty practices in the nation.

Criteria for promotion and tenure for the faculty were expanded in the 1990's to begin to recognize the clinical scholarship seen in a faculty practice program. Today, clinical scholarship is highly valued by the faculty. Many faculty regularly publish scholarly articles and book chapters based on their work in the faculty practice program.

The largest number of faculty participate in the primary care programs of the College. These include providing nurse practitioner services at various locations. The majority of the patients served by the faculty are classified as minority and either inner city or rural underserved populations. There are a number of other practices, however. The College has had a management contract with the Visiting Nurse Association for several years. The relationship with the UT Bowld Hospital continues to grow with joint education, patient care, and research activities. The chief nurse executive of the hospital serves as Assistant Dean of the College. There are joint activities with the Regional Medical Center at Memphis in the Newborn Center in which faculty provide patient care services and teach students.

There are several joint programs with the Veterans Affairs Medical Center in Memphis. These are also combined education, patient care, and research programs. Other faculty practice locations include St. Jude Children's

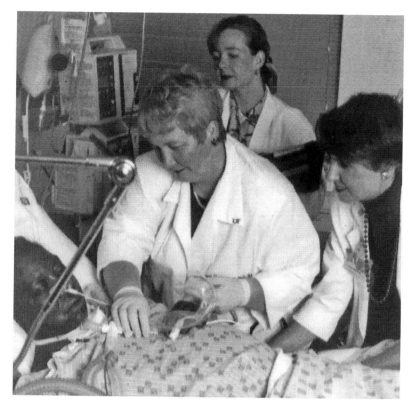

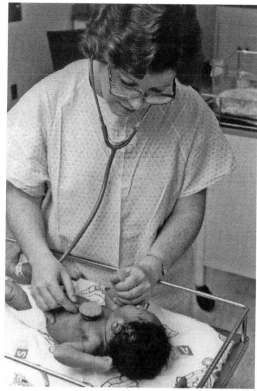

Research Hospital, Arlington Developmental Center, the Bowling Center for Developmental Disabilities, Methodist Anesthesia Group, UT Medical Group, and the Memphis and Shelby County Health Department.

Since 1993, the College of Nursing has offered the MSN with an option in anesthesia in conjunction with the UT Medical Center at Knoxville. The chief nurse executive at the Medical Center serves as Assistant Dean. Faculty who teach in this program serve in joint positions between the Medical Center and the College of Nursing.

The College is in the process of expanding its faculty practice program by opening new primary care practices in the Memphis and Shelby County area and rural Tennessee. These practices will provide needed health services to many who would have little other access while also meeting the teaching needs of the College.

As the College approaches its second century, the faculty have reclaimed their important roles joining the practice of nursing with the teaching of the next generation of nurses. Clearly, the faculty practice what they teach.

(left) Dr. Carol Thompson with graduate students Lisa Carpenter and Beth Murff caring for an intensive care patient
(right) Teresa Free, alumna and former faculty, examining newborn at THE MED

Michael A. Carter *obtained his BSN and MSN from the University of Arkansas for Medical Sciences.* ✦ *His DNSc is from Boston University. He is certified as a Family Nurse Practitioner, is a Fellow in the American Academy of Nursing and a Distinguished Practitioner in the National Academies of Practice. Before coming to UT, he was a Department Chair at the University of Colorado.* ✦ *He has served as Dean and Professor at the UT College of Nursing since 1982.* ✦

Research Program and Development of the PhD in Nursing

BY E. DIANNE GREENHILL, PROFESSOR, AND

DONNA HATHAWAY,* PROFESSOR AND DIRECTOR OF RESEARCH

The need for research, especially in the clinical areas, in the College of Nursing was identified in both the 1968 and 1976 NLN self-studies. Dean Ruth Neil Murry repeatedly encouraged research among the faculty. Non-nursing faculty were employed as consultants and teachers of nursing research courses. Dr. Ted May, a psychologist in the College of Medicine, served in the consultant role and conducted a "Longitudinal Study of Personality, Values, Attitudes and Performance of Nursing Students and Nurses." At least two publications of this research appeared in psychology journals in 1966 and 1968.

In January 1963, Dean Murry employed the first nurse in a Director of Research role. This PhD nursing faculty member was expected to conduct clinical nursing research and assist faculty in improving their competencies in research. However, for reasons that are not clear these expectations were not accomplished. According to Dean Murry's evaluation, this director was able to develop a working relationship with only two of the 20 faculty members and resigned in June 1964.

With the establishment of the graduate program in 1972, expectations were again high that the research mission would be established. The heavy teaching loads of the graduate faculty on a 12-month calendar limited opportunities.

While research remained a goal, little was accomplished until the graduate program curriculum and calendar changed under the leadership of Dean Michael Carter who aggressively

Drs. Donna Hathaway and Pamela Hinds compare clinical research notes, circa 1986

recruited faculty prepared to conduct research. As the cadre of doctorally prepared nurses at the University of Tennessee, Memphis expanded in the early 1980's, research activity became an important mission of the College of Nursing. In 1981, Dr. Sharon Scandrett-Hibdon received one of the first internally funded College of Nursing Research Awards to study the Endogenous Healing Process. Her work was subsequently funded by the American Nurses and Kellogg Foundations.

The first formal commitment to expand research at the College of Nursing into the clinical arena and establish collaborative relationships with clinical scholars came in 1984, when Dr. Donna Hathaway was hired into a 50 percent joint position with the University of Tennessee, Memphis Bowld Hospital. Shortly thereafter in 1985, Dr. Pamela Hinds joined the

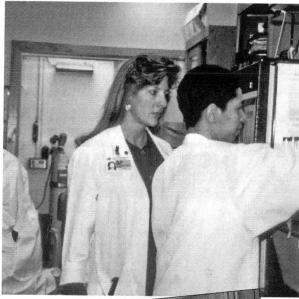

faculty in a similar position at St. Jude Children's Research Hospital.

As new doctorally prepared faculty members joined the College of Nursing who were commencing research careers, the need to support their development was recognized by the Dean who recruited and hired Dr. Mary Jane Ward as the Associate Dean for Research. Under Dr. Ward's guidance, new doctoral faculty members expanded their programs of research, sought more funding for their work, and increasingly involved students and clinicians in research activities. Dr. Ward was employed as Professor and Associate Dean for Research effective August 1, 1985. Dr. Ward's role was to develop the proposal for the PhD program and facilitate faculty research development. Dr. Ward had a major role in preparing the PhD proposal for the UT Board of Trustees which was approved in 1987. The PhD program under the Graduate College was implemented in 1988. Dr. Ward was instrumental in developing the research mission of the College and the Office of Nursing Research. During her tenure, which ended June 1988, she facilitated submission of proposals to several private foundations and at least seven proposals to federal governmental funding agencies.

The first external funds available for research in the College of Nursing came in 1987 when the college participated in a campus-wide National Institutes of Health funded project examining Health Promotion and Disease Prevention. Several faculty members conducted research as well as practice projects that spanned topics from primary care to health of the family of hospitalized patients. This project continued until 1990. The first externally funded research at the University of Tennessee, Memphis with a nursing faculty principal investigator also came after 1986 when Dr. Veronica Engle joined the faculty as the Chair of the Department of Medical-Surgical Nursing. Her study, titled "Post Relocation Health Status of Older Adults Following Nursing Home Admission," was funded by the National Institutes of Nursing Research from 1987 until 1989, and was the first of several research activities subsequently supported by the Nursing Institute.

Faculty also made use of other funding organizations to support research activities during the late 1980's. Drs. Mary Lou Shannon

(left) Dr. Donna Hathaway and Dr. S. Cardoso examine autonomic function laboratory results
(right) Doctoral students in College of Nursing Physiologic Function Laboratory established in 1996
(bottom) Dean Michael Carter and Dr. Jane Ward, Associate Dean for Research, with Miss Murry's portrait in background

(top) June 1997 PhD Nursing graduates with Dr. Hathaway, Doctoral Program Director (bottom) Dr. Melissa Faulkner testing a child for a research project

other College of Nursing faculty; other colleges on the University of Tennessee, Memphis campus; other universities; and community clinicians. Funding for research during the 1990's also increased as the College of Nursing focused its research mission on the conduct of clinical studies.

Today, research at the University of Tennessee, Memphis College of Nursing transcends the areas of health promotion, acute care, and chronicity. Health promotion research is investigating interventions which may successfully enhance the well-being of individuals in the home and community. Acute care studies are focusing on development of interventions to improve patient recovery and well-being at a time when their physical illness may require hospitalization. Studies in chronicity are examining interventions which can optimize the quality of life and quality of care for patients with chronic conditions from the hospital to formal and informal long-term care settings.

As of December 1997, the PhD Program has graduated 18 students. Dr. Michael Carter served as its first program director. Dr. Donna Hathaway is currently serving in that position and is representing nursing on the Graduate Council. June Larrabee was the first student admitted and graduated in June 1992. The student perspectives shared by June and the second graduate, Mary Hartwig, give a vivid description of the program.

and Suzanne Thomas received funding from private industry to conduct studies on the management of pressure sores and the human-environment encounter, respectively.

Several faculty members also were able to acquire funds from Sigma Theta Tau to conduct their research.

By 1990, at least two faculty members had received National Center for Nursing Research funding. One of these, Dr. Donna Hathaway, is currently serving as Director of Research and the doctoral program. The 1990's saw a maturation of the research activities in the College of Nursing. Faculty moved from conducting independent research projects to development of ongoing programs of research which involve not only students but collaborative efforts with

Donna K. Hathaway received her BSN and MS from the University of Missouri, Columbia and her PhD from the University of Texas at Austin. ♦ She was engaged in surgical nursing practice and taught in Missouri before joining the UT faculty in 1984. She is currently Professor of Nursing and Director of Clinical Transplant Research. ♦ She also is Director of the PhD Program in Nursing and Director of the Center of Nursing Research at UT. She has received numerous honors and awards for her research. ♦

Alumni Perspective: First PhD Graduate

BY JUNE HANSEN LARRABEE,* PhD. JUNE 1992

All of those affiliated with The University of Tennessee, Memphis College of Nursing can be proud of the PhD program because of the caliber of the faculty and curriculum. As I can attest, the program is designed to prepare researchers whose work is recognized by peers outside UT Memphis.

The prospect of fulfilling my lifelong dream of becoming a PhD-prepared nurse researcher largely influenced my husband's and my decision to move to Memphis from Orlando, Florida in 1987. I became an instructor in the Medical-Surgical Nursing Department and clearly communicated my interest in entering the PhD program should it be approved. A few short months after the program was approved, I was accepted as the first student. Although I knew I was to be the only student in the program for a while, I was eager to begin and appreciative of not having to wait another year.

Imagine what seminar discussion between one teacher and one student would be like! As the student, it certainly meant that I had to be prepared for each class. While this was somewhat stressful, I was highly motivated to be successful, and I enjoyed the content.

As it turned out, there were only two or three courses for which I was the only student. Arrangements were made for other faculty to participate in several of the seminar courses, enabling a greater exchange of thoughts. This was one of the ways that Michael Carter, the dean, Veronica Engle, my department chair, and the other two department

June Larrabee, doctoral student, 1990

chairs, Carol Panicucci and Kaye Engelhardt, intervened to minimize the potential stresses of my being the sole student.

During the first year of my program, Margaret (Peg) Hartig transferred into the program, and we had the good fortune of being classmates for a number of courses. Our diverse backgrounds enriched our interactions as we shared differing perspectives on issues and learned from each other's experiences. Personally, we commiserated over shared challenges which we will always treasure.

My learning experience was further enhanced by interactions with students in the second PhD class. Their unique professional and personal experiences often led to diverse insights and queries that expanded the group's thinking. Similar benefit arose from participation in seminar discussions by experienced research faculty. Much of my knowledge about research was acquired through learning how different faculty members orchestrated their research projects and their research program.

My memories of the PhD student experience encompass all dimensions of my life. While I was a full-time student, I worked half-time as the Nursing Care Quality Manager at the Regional Medical Center at Memphis. Certainly, the demands on my time and attention created coping challenges for my husband and teenage daughter that they would not otherwise have had to face. For instance, I clearly remember working 77 straight days to recruit participants into my dissertation research study. Both husband and daughter acquired new culinary talents as a by-product of my education!

For the most part, I engaged in a balancing act throughout the program to meet the demands of the educational experience and my job and to meet the needs of my family — a scenario shared by most adult learners. Also like other adult learners, I had the benefit of being actively encouraged and enabled by others to succeed. During the time I was developing the beginnings of my theoretical model of quality, I was thinking about all the factors that could interact to influence completion of

$$LOT=f[PXx[(SH/TxNT)xHR]+PPT=3(EDT)+NS+PB]$$
$$PI+GS+PEF+PED+PS+SOS+SE+OCB$$

CODE:

f = function of

NUMERATOR TERMS:	DENOMINATOR TERMS:
PX = Personal expenses	PI = Personal income
SH/T = Semester hrs. in term	GS = Grant support
NT = Number of terms	PEF = Professional encouragement from faculty
HR = Hours required	PED = Professional encouragement from Dean
PPT = Proposal prep. time	PS = Peer support
EDT = Est. dissertation time	SOS = Sig. others support
NS = Number of subjects	SE = Self esteem
PB = Perfectionistic behavior	OCB = Obsessive compulsive behavior

the program. Flights of fancy led me to create, for the fun of it, the model above: Larrabee's Model of Doctoral Student's Length of Time (LOT) to Graduation.

This model's utility is limited to comic

relief for stressed-out doctoral students who may identify additional variables for the numerator and denominator and thus, use humor for its personal therapeutic value! Academically, the major limitation of this model is that it is based on a mechanistic atomism world-view, and therefore, inconsistent with the holistic underpinnings of nursing.

Seriously though, the various support factors within the above denominator were very real for me throughout my doctoral program. I always appreciated the fact that the dean and faculty admitted students whom they thought had a good chance of successfully completing the program. To adequately prepare researchers with a strong theoretical and research repertoire, the faculty designed the curriculum to be rigorous and had high expectations of the students. However, throughout my program I felt that I was living in an optimistic academic milieu. I perceived the faculty to anticipate that I could be successful and frequently felt "cheered-on" by both course faculty and faculty not involved in the doctoral program. Similarly, I felt that many of my peers at the hospital were boosters of my progress through the program, especially Marie Ray Knight, the Vice President for Patient Care Services, to whom I reported.

As one might anticipate, the members of my dissertation committee had the greatest influence on my development as a researcher (and on my LOT!). Dr. Cyril Chang opened my eyes to the reality of health care economics. Dr. Carol Thompson helped me clarify concepts in my theoretical model and model for investigation by her tenacious objective critique, and she was a stalwart booster of my progress. Dr. Elizabeth Tolley patiently and enthusiastically helped me learn to enjoy, not fear, Biostatistics and to develop some measure of confidence in conducting statistical analyses. Dr. Michael Carter's suggestions and consistent belief in my ability were key factors in my daring to develop a theoretical model of quality while a

(left) June Larrabee preparing final copy of dissertation with Dr. Carter and Dr. Veronica Engle, Dissertation Chair (right) Dr. Larrabee with Dissertation Committee at Completion of Defense!

student. This work was later judged by external peer reviewers to be worthy of publication in *Image: Journal of Nursing Scholarship.* As my dissertation chairperson, Dr. Veronica Engle had incomparable influence on my development as a researcher. Although I learned much from her in the courses she taught, I learned a tremendous amount from interacting with her during my directed study and dissertation. She was an excellent role model for methodical, detailed planning of research design and conduct. Through Dr. Engle's critique of numerous revisions of my dissertation chapters, I acquired improved skill in scientific writing. The research I conducted under her direction was later judged by external peer reviewers to be worthy of publication in the international journal *Scandinavian Journal of Caring Sciences.* Beyond her role as dissertation chairperson, Dr. Engle was sensitive to my experience as student and was continuously supportive and encouraging. Support from my family, encouragement and guidance from my dissertation committee members were key factors in my successful, timely completion of the program.

As a consequence of this program, I am living one of my life dreams — conducting research. Now, I have the necessary skills to design and conduct both quantitative and qualitative studies. Through continued experience and learning, I anticipate building those skills. Also, I anticipate continuing development of the model of quality because it may serve as a framework for better understanding and improving health care quality. I am gratified to have acquired these skills and proud to be a graduate of The University of Tennessee, Memphis PhD in Nursing program.

*June Hansen Larrabee received her BSN from Medical College of Georgia, her MS from Boston University and her PhD in Nursing from UT in 1992. ✦ She held positions in Florida and Georgia as a clinical nurse specialist and faculty prior to joining UT faculty in 1987. She currently is Research Scientist, Camcare Institute: Center for Nursing Research in Charleston, West Virginia. ✦

Alumni Perspective

BY MARY HARTWIG,* PhD. JUNE 1993

Personal Background

The opening of the Nursing PhD program at UT Memphis was something I had anticipated for at least 10 years prior to the event. For me it was a giant step because my last formal education had been completed 22 years previously, and some of my background knowledge, especially in the biological sciences, needed updating. In addition, my computer skills were rudimentary and I had not used any but the most elementary statistics in years. Another hurdle was that my college entrance test scores were outdated or lost, or both, and I had to retake the Graduate Record Exam before being considered for admission. Finally, though, in the spring of 1989, with my GRE scores in hand, I journeyed from Jonesboro, Arkansas to Memphis for an interview with a faculty committee: Veronica Engle, Donna Hathaway and Leon McAulay.

In the course of that interview, it became clear that doctoral students are expected to take an active role in planning their educational experiences, to have their goals well delineated, and to prepare for complete immersion in their research. What changes I had to make in my approach to education! I was also invited to attend Pam Hinds' qualitative research class that day, joining my soon-to-be classmates, June Larrabee and Peg Hartig, who were the first two PhD students admitted to the program. Following the class, I was hooked, though somewhat overwhelmed by the volume of reading required. My doctoral program (1989-1993), had a life-changing impact on me, memories of which I can best organize into three themes: *content, competencies* and *scholar's role.*

PROGRAM IMPACT
Content

Cognate area. Within established guidelines for selecting didactic course content, each student was expected to develop a course of studies in a cognate area that would best enhance and complement his or her skills as a nurse scholar. With the help and urging of Dean Michael Carter, I selected neuroscience, offered through the UT Memphis Department of Neuroanatomy. Given the complexity of the subject matter and the fact that my background knowledge was outdated, there were many moments when I was sure that I could not tolerate one more lecture on rat brain tract tracing, keep straight all the newly discovered neurotransmitters and their actions, or figure out the electrophysiology of the cell membrane. However, Dr. Carter's unflagging "can-do" attitude and the support and encouragement of the neuroscience faculty helped me through the 12 hours of neuroscience course work. That content has been invaluable to me, not only in understanding pharmacology and immunology mechanisms in an entirely different way, but also in developing the graduate-level pathophysiology course which I have taught for several semesters. I will never forget Dr. Bill Crowley's explanation of how caffeine blocks adenosine receptors, thus increasing one's alertness, or Dr. Steve Kitai's memorable cerebellum lecture, in which he explained why cats cannot play the piano! Another benefit of my neuroscience course work was the contact with bench scientists, and the opportunity to interpret to them the insights and experiences of a clinically oriented scientist.

Research

From the very first days of Dr. Carter's "Philosophy of Science" course, we learned that scholars must be aware of their own world view, which will influence their underlying assumptions and frame the very questions they ask. Fellow students Carol Dobos, Cheryl Stegbauer and I discovered that clarifying concepts and analyzing how they would be studied under various philosophical orientations was a mind-bending, frustrating, despair-producing, but ultimately exhilarating experience. When Susan Jacob, Judy Martin and Debbie Crom took the course the next year, they seemed to be doing a lot more laughing in class than we had done, but they assured me it was just hysterics!

Because Nursing is an eclectic discipline, asking questions ranging from the "what is it?" to the "how can I make it happen?" type, we took courses in nonempirical as well as empirical approaches to research. Dr. Roni Engle finally got through to me how to ask crisp, clear research questions, and Dr. Pam Hinds opened my eyes to the rigor, complexity, and excitement of the phenomenological method. I will always be grateful for having been required to conduct, present and publish both quantitative and qualitative research in my doctoral program at UTM, because my professional work has required skills in both methods of inquiry.

Competencies

It was obvious that Ph.D. curriculum planners had a clear understanding that

Dr. Mary Hartwig

certain competencies were essential to becoming modern nurse scholars. In addition, they understood that acquiring these competencies required meaningful practice as well as access to experts who could provide guidance and necessary feedback as novices learned the skills of scholarly inquiry. That kind of expertise was readily available to doctoral students through the cooperative arrangements made by the College of Nursing with statisticians, computer specialists, and health care practitioners in other fields within the University. Dr. Sergio Cardoso generously made his autonomic function testing laboratory and records available to me, and taught me so much about the relative merits of the cardiovascular and vascular response tests in assessing autonomic function. He has remained a mentor. I remember, gratefully, the many hours of calm, patient assistance given me by biostatistician Dr. Betsy Tolley. She helped me understand and interpret the endless pages of computer printouts generated for my various research projects, and made

Dr. Mary Hartwig (far right) and other UT College of Nursing Kellogg Post-Doctoral fellows in primary care, 1997

me marvel at the ease with which she could find and help me correct glitches in my SAS commands while working on the VAX. And to this day, I use a method Dr. Steve Kritchevsky, also of the Biostatistics Department, taught me for remembering specificity, sensitivity, and positive/negative predictive values.

But in addition to the specific skills learned in the other fields of Medicine and Biostatistics, the College of Nursing provided an environment in which doctoral students were permitted to ask questions, share ideas, and practice their new roles as nursing scholars. We had individual offices complete with computers connected to the University's centralized computer system and full access to the University's library system. We did not have e-mail or Internet access then, but I can just imagine what a boon that is to today's doctoral students as they try to keep up with the literature in their field. The entire faculty and staff willingly helped me with all questions, whether trivial or time-consuming; everyone seemed oriented to the notion of helping students learn and produce good work.

Scholar's Role

The third theme of my doctoral program memories is that of learning the scholar's role. Efforts of the graduate nursing faculty seemed to be focused on that theme, and I was fortunate enough to be able to live that process as a graduate research assistant and full member of the Transplant Department Research Team. That two-year experience is where I gained my fullest appreciation of what it means to be a member of an active clinical research team, with responsibility for quality patient care as well as study of outcomes. Contributions from all members of the team were expected and accepted, and it was as a member of that team that I first actually practiced research and was required to think like a researcher on a daily basis. Dr. Donna Hathaway, chair of my dissertation committee, was my mentor and guide as I worked my way through the maze of data being collected on quality of life. She could quickly clear up my "fuzzy" questions, suggest ways to solve data collection problems, and cut through red tape to gain access to clinical data. And always, she kept before me the notion that part of planning the research project was planning dissemination of the findings through presentations and publications. We continue to work together.

Other invaluable experiences in the program were writing a research grant proposal as a course requirement, and being involved in preparing evaluation materials for a funded grant project. From both of these, I learned the value of interdisciplinary team work, and the importance of professional networking and collaboration. Finally, I had the privilege of having my oral and written work critiqued by superb academics and clinicians such as Dr. Hathaway, Dr. Tolley, Dr. Carol Thompson (Nursing) and Dr. A. Osama Gaber (Transplant Surgery Department). They insisted on straightforward, unambiguous expression of ideas, avoidance of hackneyed terms, and the development and consistent usage of well-defined concepts. Whenever my students bemoan my copious red-pencil marks on their papers, I just assure them that the best way to learn good writing is to have your work carefully edited. It helps to speak as one who has been there!

Though I have organized my memories of the doctoral program under three themes, they do not completely capture all the images I have of my years at UT Memphis. Those images form a collage:

• The 75-mile commutes late at night or early in the morning.

• The pride of my family, contrasted with my guilt feelings for not spending enough time with them.

• The camaraderie with a young UT Memphis faculty member whose office was just across the hall from mine, and who was concurrently completing her dissertation at Wayne State University. Her encouragement and always upbeat attitude were wonderfully supportive, and I take great pride now in calling her my friend and colleague, Dr. Mona Wicks.

• The wonderful support of younger classmates in the program, and the special bond with Cheryl Johnson, with whom I share a birthday.

• Attending research conferences with doctoral program classmates in Tucson, Arizona; Chicago, Illinois; and Chattanooga, Tennessee.

• The tediousness of collecting data on organ donors in a medical records department, along with the sobering realization that the majority of these died due to self-inflicted violence.

• The delight of patients who received a successful organ transplantation, and the pain and grief of those who experienced organ rejection. And consistently, the gratitude for a second chance at a better life, and the desire to help others through participation in our research.

• The joy of everyone when someone on the team had a paper or poster accepted at a convention, or a manuscript accepted for publication.

• The despair of losing hours of valuable thinking time at the computer because there was a power glitch and I had not enacted the automatic "save" feature.

• The gentle cajoling by Dr. Michael Carter to just focus on my dissertation and get it completed: "We do not have a position called Student Emeritus," he told me on more than one occasion.

And so I did complete and defend my dissertation in January 1993, graduating in the June 4, 1993 commencement ceremony as the second Nursing PhD from UT Memphis. I will always remember the generosity of faculty and staff in helping me complete my course requirements, the support and encouragement of the faculty and transplant team, and the superb resources of the University of Tennessee made available to me in the doctoral program.

*Mary S. Hartwig *received her BSN from the University of Minnesota and her MN from the University of Washington. She has been a faculty member and was Chair of the Nursing Program at Arkansas State University from 1993-1997.* ✦ *She is a Professor at ASU and adjunct Professor at the University of Arkansas for Medical Sciences. In 1997 she completed a W.K. Kellogg Post Doctoral Faculty Fellowship in Primary Care at UT Memphis College of Nursing. She currently holds the position of Director of Nursing Education, Area Health Education Center, North East Arkansas.* ✦

People, Places, Events

Orren Williams Hyman, PhD (1890-1968)

Dr. O.W. Hyman, U.T. Campus Administrator, circa 1960

Dr. O.W. Hyman was a part of the University of Tennessee Medical Units for 48 years. He came to Memphis as an Assistant Professor in histology and embryology in September 1913. He left UT to earn his PhD at Princeton University and returned in 1921 with the title of Registrar-Burser. According to the alumni publication, Center-Grams, there were only three buildings at UT — Eve, Lindsley, and Rogers Halls — when Dr. Hyman arrived. By the time of his retirement June 30, 1961, there was an extensive Medical Units campus with colleges and schools of Medicine, Dentistry, Pharmacy, Nursing, Biological Sciences, and Graduate Programs. Dr. Hyman's strong leadership brought about this transformation. He held various titles over the years, including Business Manager, Administrative Officer of the Colleges in Memphis, Dean of the College of Medicine, and Dean of Administration. Regardless of title, Dr. Hyman was the chief administrative officer for the Memphis campus. From 1949-1961, he was Vice President in charge of the UT Medical Units. Honors included appointment by President Truman in 1951 to the National Science Foundation Board of Directors and named the Newspaper Guild's Memphis "Man of the Year" in 1953. The Hyman Administration Building was opened in 1955 and named in his honor.

Frank June Montgomery (1907-2007)

Mr. Frank June Montgomery Director of Alumni Affairs, 1970

June Montgomery came to the UT Medical Units on June 8, 1936, serving in a variety of roles related to student services. The University purchased the Rex Club on the corner of Madison and Dunlap in 1935 and renovated it to be the University Center. Mr. Montgomery was hired as assistant student welfare secretary to direct the activities of the Center. He served as bookstore manager until a full-time manager was appointed around 1961, as dormitory manager until 1946, and Director of Student Affairs until 1969. He started the intramural program in 1937 and organized many other student activities.

"During the 1940's and 1950's when students particularly were struggling financially, June Montgomery offered financial aid, part-time jobs, encouragement, and advice. Mr. Montgomery set the standard for personal interest and love of people that makes students feel at home when away from home and nourishes high regard for one's Alma Mater." (Hamner, 1986, pp. 93-94).

A medical student loan fund was established in his honor by the College of Medicine. The major organization of alumni activities for the Medical Units is credited to Mr. Montgomery. He served as Director of Alumni Affairs from 1941 until his retirement on August 31, 1973. He still attends alumni activities and maintains contacts with alumni throughout the United States.

Jim Stockdale, "The Coach Who Nursed Basketball Fever for 26 Years"

TAKEN FROM AN APRIL 28, 1988 *COMMERCIAL APPEAL* COLUMN WRITTEN BY AL DUNNING AND REPRINTED IN THE *NURSING ALUMNI MAGAZINE*, FALL 1988

Few college-level basketball coaches unleashed as many killer teams as Jim Stockdale did... He had 20 winning seasons, three undefeated teams and a lifetime record of 333-151.

Listen to Shirley Stagner, the director of quality of life services at the Memphis Cancer Center and captain of the UT Nurses squad in 1969-70: "Years after I graduated, I talked about Coach Stockdale as the most special person I had ever known in all my life. He inspired all of us who were fortunate enough to have come in contact with him."

Shucks, Stockdale said, it was he who was the lucky one. "Coaching the team was strictly an avocation. My job was not connected to basketball in any way. It (coaching) was just something I wanted to do. So I always felt I had the very best of worlds in coaching. I did not have to worry about recruiting or alumni pressure, and the only time I had to worry about the won-lost record was when I felt I had not done the job as I should have..."

A native of Knoxville, Stockdale aspired to be a high school basketball coach. That remained his goal after he graduated from Oberlin College and entered graduate school at the University of Tennessee. During his last year of postgraduate studies, he realigned his career gunsights.

"I got an offer in what looked like a fascinating career — and one that was a little more stable than coaching," he said. That offer came from the University of Tennessee itself. He became director of student welfare at the

1960 Basketball Champions

(top) Jim Stockdale and UT Nurses team watch tournament events (bottom) Basketball action in UT Gym

Tennessee medical school in Memphis in the fall of 1955.

Shortly after he arrived, school brass asked him to find a coach for the student nurses' basketball team. He said, "How about me?" It was the start of a good thing that lasted until 1981, when an illness forced Stockdale to give up coaching... he remains at the school as assistant to the vice chancellor for facilities and human resources.

Stockdale's first teams played in the old Park Commission Nurses' League against rivals like those from St. Joseph, Baptist and Methodist hospitals. "We played about 12 games a year at the time. You did not read much about it in the paper, but it really mattered for those who were playing."

In Stockdale's second season, 1956-57, they started a nurses' tournament called the Cotton States Nurses Invitational. "It took off like a rocket." Soon it was drawing teams from

Indiana, Kentucky, Georgia, Alabama, Kansas, Arkansas... It was the golden age of Mid-South nurses' basketball. But it was doomed.

The UT Nurses team folded after the 1985 season — a victim of the times, Stockdale said. Nursing schools had changed. And so had women's basketball.

Today's nursing students tend to be older, more family-oriented, Stockdale said. Many are commuters. The proliferation of nursing schools has spread students more thinly... and a growing percentage of nursing students are male. Women's basketball, meanwhile, has gone big time.

Stockdale's UT Nurses teams won seven Cotton States titles. They were champs of the Nurses League 12 times. Yet the victories never impressed the coach that much; he did not know his lifetime record until Wednesday when *The Commercial Appeal* added it up.

"I do not want to go corny on you, but it is difficult to sit here and describe what all those years meant to those girls and to me. It was more than just having a good ball club."

"The Closing of John Gaston"

BY DAVID DAWSON, REPRINTED IN PART FROM THE *NURSING ALUMNI MAGAZINE*, FALL 1988

On May 10 of this year, the curtain finally fell on John Gaston Hospital. It had been over six years since the hospital had patients, and close to two years since the building was cleared of office space.

Yet there were many who came to a special ceremony last spring to remember the contributions of this once-grand hospital, and to celebrate the nearly 52 years of service which John Gaston Memorial Hospital provided to the community. However sound it was in its prime, during the last decade of its life, John Gaston had fallen into disrepair. Although never unclean, it had quite simply become threadbare, especially when compared with the well-equipped private hospitals springing up in Memphis' suburban neighborhoods. Despite its reputation as a slightly run-down facility (many liken John Gaston to TV's *St. Elsewhere*)..., the effect of this hospital on Memphis' overall medical community remains immeasurable.

A major reason of this lies in the fact that John Gaston served as the University of Tennessee, Memphis' primary training ground for generations of physicians, nurses, dentists, pharmacists, and other health professionals. Here in this teaching hospital, Memphis's medical community was introduced to many of the new techniques and new technologies developed during the past half century.

Among the many firsts at John Gaston were the South's first intensive care unit; the nation's first sickle cell anemia treatment unit; one of the nation's first artificial kidney machines; the South's first blood bank; a precursor to The Med's Trauma Center; and the city's first organ transplants and kidney dialysis...

While John Gaston had its physical beginnings during the midst of the Great Depression,

its roots date back to 1829, when the state's first hospital was chartered... In 1936 the John Gaston was built. It served as both the city's public hospital and a teaching facility for the University of Tennessee College of Medicine.

What still surprises people is that the man for whom the hospital is named had no medical connections. Instead of being a noted doctor, John Gaston was a noted chef who owned some of the city's finest restaurants and hotels on Court Square in the years just after the Civil War. Gaston died in 1912, at the age of 84. When his widow died in 1929, her will revealed that Gaston had requested $300,000 of his estate be used to build a hospital at their home. When the Gaston home proved far too small for a modern hospital, the city added Gaston's bequest to city and federal funds, and came up with around $800,000 to build the John Gaston Hospital on the site of the old Memphis General.

The new six-story, 550 bed hospital was dedicated on June 27, 1936. Designed to be a public hospital, John Gaston's four floors of wards served primarily indigent patients. Less than five percent of those who entered the hospital were paying patients who sought specialized services.

But the lack of paying patients did not hinder the hospital's staff from energetically tackling many of the medical problems of the day. From its inception John Gaston was "an outstanding center for treatment and research," says Lemuel W. Diggs, a physician who served as chief of the hospital's laboratories from

John Gaston Hospital

opening day until his retirement in 1969. "The only trouble is that nobody outside the hospital knew, even back then, all the important things that went on at John Gaston." For instance, Diggs says that he noticed Memphis had the highest mortality rate for new mothers in the country during the late 1930's. "Women who had just given birth were bleeding to death because we did not have any blood to give them," he says. "We had to do a blood type, and then hunt all over the place for a donor, and by that time the woman was usually dead." To meet this challenge, Diggs organized — through private contributions — the first blood bank in the South, which opened simultaneously with the first in the nation...

In the mid-1950's, John Gaston Hospital began to be surrounded with newer, specialized facilities. In 1956, the E.H. Crump Hospital was built to serve black patients. (Although John Gaston had always treated blacks, Crump Hospital was built to compensate for the fact that private hospital care was nearly nonexistent for black Memphians.) In 1957, the Tobey wing was added. Six years later the Walter Chandler

Clinical Services Center opened, followed in 1965 by the William F. Bowld Hospital. By that time, John Gaston Hospital was no longer the main public hospital; it was, instead, part of a vast treatment, training, and research complex. In 1964, John Gaston merged with E. H. Crump as the City of Memphis Hospitals, and in 1970 the complex became known simply as City of Memphis Hospital. Although several of these hospitals remain open today under the auspices of the Regional Medical Center at Memphis, John Gaston's tenure is finished.

When dignitaries, former staff and patients, and a handful of bystanders gathered at the hospital for the last time this spring, the mood was one of pride tinged with sadness. "People should not forget that here was one of the outstanding hospitals in the country," says Jim Gibb Johnson. "Although it never got the recognition it deserved, John Gaston did a tremendous job of educating students, caring for patients, and providing research. It was one of the giants."

Beta Theta Chapter at Large, Sigma Theta Tau International Honor Society of Nursing

The BSN class of 1967 gave the College of Nursing funds to establish a local Honor Society. Upsilon Tau was established in May 1970 with membership extended to nurses and students who demonstrated academic excellence and leadership. This organization became the basis for the Beta Theta Chapter of Sigma Theta Tau which was chartered at UT on May 20, 1972 with 118 charter inductees, 10 of whom transferred from other chapters. Shirley Stagner was the first president. Other officers in 1972 included Jean Lancaster, Fay Russell, Rachel Taylor, Dorothy Griscom, Jean Arnold and Sarah Mynatt. In 1982 the newsletter, Beta Theta Data, was published for the first time and continues at this time. On May 7, 1988, the honor society was rechartered as Beta Theta

Chapter at Large including both the University of Tennessee College of Nursing and Memphis State University School of Nursing (now University of Memphis). Sigma Theta Tau has as its purposes to recognize superior achievement and the development of leadership qualities, to foster high professional standards, encourage creative work, and to strengthen commitments to the ideals and purposes of the profession. Undergraduate students from both institutions and graduate students from UT are inducted into the society semiannually. Beta Theta Chapter at Large awards scholarships and research grants to its members and sponsors a research conference each year.

UT College of Nursing Alumni Association

The College of Nursing Alumni Association represents more than 4,000 graduates from our college and is an integral part of the University of Tennessee National Alumni Association. The association gives an award annually to a graduating senior and graduate student who demonstrates excellence in clinical nursing. This award presented at the annual alumni day and recognized at graduation is a seal to be placed on the diploma.

The class of 1965 established an award to an undergraduate first-year student for outstanding achievement in the areas of scholastic ability, professional interest, and leadership potential. This award of $50.00 was continued annually by the Alumni Association. The Outstanding Alumnus and Most Supportive Alumnus awards are presented annually by the Alumni Association.

The Board of Directors meets at least two times each year with the Dean. This group comprises active supporters of the College and promote fundraising. Endowed scholarships supported by the alumni and friends of the College are the Ruth Neil Murry Scholarship, named in honor of the College's late dean; the Grace Spice Wallace Scholarship, and the Marie Buckley Scholarship. Endowed visiting professorships established as a part of the 21st Century Capital Campaign are the Beverly H. Bowns, the Mary L. Morris, and the Elinor F. Reed Distinguished Visiting Professorships. All three were influential faculty members at the College.

Alumni Day luncheon reunion

Appendices

Rules for Student Nurses

FROM MERTIE B. HENDERSON LONG, CLASS OF 1944

1. Reasonable quiet must be maintained at all times. Absolute quiet after 10:00 p.m. All radios off at 10:00 p.m.

2. All students except those on late leaves must be in their own rooms by 10:00 p.m. No baths may be taken after 10:00 p.m.

3. The students in rooms on third floor may have radios. Radios must be off by 10:00 p.m. Radios must not be played loudly enough to disturb neighbors.

4. The student's name must be placed on the door of her room. Rooms must be kept neat and orderly at all times. Bath rooms are to be left clean.

5. Students are not to take relatives to their rooms without permission from the housemother.

6. Students must wear housecoats or kimonos in the halls of the home. Shades must be down while dressing.

7. Students are not to make or receive telephone calls after 10:00 p.m. Students off duty are never to call students on duty or vice versa. No long distance calls or telegrams are to be put in over the telephones in the residence.

8. Roll call at 6:30 a.m. every day except Sunday. All students must attend except those on night duty or diet service. Those having morning hours must sign for them in the residence office. Students are not to return to their rooms after roll call.

9. Night nurses leave the home at 10:30 p.m. Night nurses are expected to spend at least eight hours per day in bed.

10. Late leave and all night leaves.
    A. First year students.
    1. One 11:30 leave on Saturday nights, providing their grades are satisfactory.
    2. Must be in the home by 10:00 p.m. on Sunday and Wednesday nights.
    3. Must be in the home by 8:00 p.m. on Mondays, Tuesdays, Thursdays, and Fridays.
    4. Secure permission for all leaves from Miss Cunningham.

    B. Second year students.
    1. One 11:30 leave on Wednesday or Saturday nights. Sign out in the residence office before 8:00 p.m.
    2. Must be in home by 10:00 p.m. except when having late leaves.
    3. Any second year student not making satisfactory grades will be placed on first year regulations.

    C. Third year students.
    1. Two 11:30 leaves per week, one on Wednesday and one on Saturday nights. Sign out in residence before 8:00 p.m.
    2. Must be in home by 10:00 p.m. every night, except the nights have late leaves.
    3. Any third year student not making satisfactory grades will be placed on first year regulations.

D. All students.

1. No late leaves will be granted on Sunday nights.
2. Late leaves will not be granted on Monday or Tuesday nights, unless student is relieving on the Ward on Wednesday night. No late leaves on Thursday or Friday nights, unless relieving on Saturday nights. Secure permit slip from housemother and take to the Nursing School Office before 5:00 p.m.
3. Night nurses may have two 10:30 leaves per week, on Wednesday and Saturday nights. No 11:30 leaves.
4. Special permission may be secured on weeknights for concerts, plays, etc. of cultural or educational value.

E. 1:30 leaves

1. Will not be granted to any students whose grades are not satisfactory.
2. Replaces a regular late leave, not in addition to them.
3. Will be granted only for University functions. These functions must be scheduled with Mr. Haney, as official school functions.
4. Not more than two per month.
5. Secure permit slip from house-mother and take to the nursing school office before 5:00 p.m.

All night leaves:

1. To obtain an all night leave the Nursing School Office must have a letter from the student's parent requesting such a privilege be granted.
2. Will not be granted in place of a 1:30 leave.
3. Cannot be obtained the same week a 1:30 leave has been granted.

11. Illness

1. Any illness must be reported to the Nursing School Office immediately.
2. Students returning on duty after an absence or illness must report the Nursing School Office.
3. No student off duty due to illness may be out of the home without permission, nor may she be granted a late leave.
4. Reasonable safeguarding of health is expected of all students. This includes appropriate use of hats, capes, raincoats, galoshes, umbrellas, etc.

12. Uniforms

1. The uniform is to be worn only on the ground of the hospital and university and adjacent areas.
2. Uniform dress must be 12 inches from the floor and aprons 11 inches from floor.
3. White hose and plain white oxfords having white heels with rubber caps must be worn. Hose must be above the knees.
4. A watch with a second hand, a fountain pen, and a pair of bandage scissors constitute a part of the prescribed uniform.
5. Uniforms must be clean and neat at all times.
6. Hair must be arranged neatly and up off the collar of the uniform. If long, or likely to come down, wear a hair net.
7. No jewelry or excessive cosmetics are to be worn with the uniform.

13. Laundry

1. Laundry must be securely tied in a bag and dropped down the laundry chute before 10:00 p.m. Sunday nights.
2. Each article must be legibly marked with the owner's name in indelible ink or name tape.
3. Silk articles or articles small enough to be easily lost are not to be sent to the laundry.
4. Students get their clean laundry from the linen room between 12:30 and 5:00 p.m. on Thursdays and Saturdays. Night nurses may get theirs between 7:30 and 8:00 a.m. Thursdays and Saturdays.

14. Students are not permitted to visit in the hospital when off duty.

1. Students desiring to visit a sick nurse or friend in the hospital must secure written permission from the Nursing School Office.
2. Students wishing to show visitors through the hospital must secure permission from the Nursing School Office.
3. When on duty students are never to leave the ward on which they are working except for necessary errands.

15. Nurses are urged to attend the church of their choice regularly.

Churches near the hospital are:

Bellevue Baptist, 28 N. Bellevue

St. Mary's Cathederal, 714 Poplar

First Baptist, 538 Linden

Grace Episcopal Church, 23 S. Manassas

St. Peter's Catholic, 1940 Adams

Madison Heights Methodist, 22 S.Claybrook

East End Christian, 1821 Peabody

Church of Christ, Union & Tucker

First Methodist, 200 N. 2nd St.

First Presbyterian Church, 175 Poplar

A list of all the churches of the city may be found in the back of the telephone directory.

Sources

The Army Nurse Corps. (1901, January). *American Journal of Nursing*. 1. 881-882.

Brown, E.L. (1948). *Nursing for the Future*. New York: Russell Sage Foundation.

The Commercial Appeal. 1897-1977. Memphis, TN.

Four workers retire after long service in extension, (1946, September). *Tennessee Extension Review*, 30, 1, 3.

Goodale, H.C. (1949). National planning for Nursing and Nursing education, In *Fifty-fifth annual report of the National League of Nursing Education* (pp. 227-232). New York: NLNE.

Hamner, J.E. (1986). *The University of Tennessee, Memphis 75th Anniversary-Medical Accomplishments*. Memphis: The University of Tennessee.

Hyman, O.W. Correspondence & files. Memphis, TN. University of Tennessee.

Kalisch. P.A. & Kalisch, B.J. (1986). *The Advance of American Nursing*. Boston: Little, Brown.

Keller, M. (1970). *Occupational Health Content in Baccalaureate Nursing Education*. Cincinnati: US Bureau of Occupational Safety and Health.

La Point. P.M. (1984). *From Saddlebags to Science: A century of health care in Memphis 1830-1930*. Memphis: University of Tennessee Center for the Health Sciences Printing Services.

Ledger lines. (1887, December 5). *Memphis Public Ledger*.

Memphis General Hospital School of Nursing Bulletin (1926). Memphis, TN.

Murry, R.N. Correspondence & files. Memphis, TN: University of Tennessee College of Nursing.

Murry, R.N. (1961). From a Diploma to a Baccalaureate Program in Nursing. *Nursing Outlook*. 9(8), 503-504.

Norman, E. & Elfried, S. (1995). How did they all survive? An analysis of American nurses' experiences in Japanese prisoner-of-war camps. *Nursing History Review*, 3, 105-127.

Norman, E. & Elfried, S. (1993). The Angels of Bataan. *Image*, 25(2), 121-126.

Nursing Schools – Today and Tomorrow. (1934). Final Report of the Committee on the Grading of Nursing Schools, New York.

Roberts, M. (1954). *American Nursing: History and Interpretation*. New York: Macmillan.

Schmidt, Imogene Kennedy. Personal Communications. August 10, 1993 & December 1, 1993.

Stewart, M.J. & Black, W.T. eds. (1971). *History of Medicine in Memphis*. Jackson, TN: McCowat-Mercer.

The United States Cadet Nurse Corps and Other Federal Nurse Training Programs, 1943-1948. (1950). Federal Security Agency, US Public Health Service Publication #38. Washington: US Government Printing Office.

University of Tennessee Board of Trustees Minutes, 1926-1962. UT Knoxville archives.

University of Tennessee Record. Biennial Report of the Board of Trustees. 1924-1926, 1928-1930. University of Tennessee Press.

University of Tennessee School of Nursing and Medical Units Bulletins 1927-1970.

University of Tennessee Medical Units and The University of Tennessee, Memphis General Catalogs 1972-1996.

Warner, L.A. (1903, January). Experience of an Army Nurse in Cuba. *Memphis Medical Monthly*, 23, 191-196.

Warner, L.A. (1899-1902). Correspondence. (Military records group 112, document file 70920). Washington, DC: National Archives.

Warner, L. (1919-1941). Annual Reports. (Tennessee University Agricultural Extension Service Reports). Knoxville, TN: University of Tennessee Archives.

West, M. & Hawkins, C. (1950). *Nursing Schools at the Mid-Century*. New York: National Committee for the Improvement of Nursing Services.

Wooten, N.E., & Williams, G . (1955). *A History of the Tennessee State Nurses' Association*. Nashville: TSNA.

Zalabak, D. (1975). *Highlights in the History of the Army Nurse Corps*. Washington, D.C.: US Army Medical Department.